CONNECTING
WITH YOUR TEENS

Fun, simple and practical ideas to
help raise resilient teenagers

Andy McNeilly

Praise for *Connecting with Your Teens*

Not often do you find a parenting book that is easy to read and relatable, especially when life is so full and hectic. The chapter themes and ideas to create discussion are realistic and practical. Andy shares his stories and others to illustrate some really typical, sensible, potential and teachable moments to help inform and guide parents and grandparents today with reflections from the past and present.

Gail McHardy, CEO, Parents Victoria Inc.

Sometimes it's hard to see the wood for the trees when parenting, particularly in this current environment so unfamiliar to our generation. Andy's 'pearls of parenting wisdom' can really help you with simple strategies to approach the hardest, yet most rewarding job we have – parenting.

Katie, mother of three teenagers

You won't find a humbler guy with a genuine passion for the resilience and wellness of our children and their families. An educator of unique storytelling ability, Andy shares experiences that will resonate with many and remind us we are not alone, and help is at hand.

Andrew, father of three teenagers

Andy's book offers parents ways to effectively engage their teenagers with unique concepts and easy activities. It was refreshing not to read another book that only focused on how teens think. Excellent activities for the entire family, its exactly what most parents need in their parenting toolbox!

Renee, mother of two teenagers

What a great format for a book, great concepts and great ideas to help engage with our teens! Uncomplicated ideas and thoroughly usable techniques to get the conversations happening, well done Andy!

Hugh, father and stepfather of five teenagers

Published in 2023 by Amba Press, Melbourne, Australia
www.ambapress.com.au

© Andy McNeilly 2023

All rights reserved. No part of this book may be reproduced or transmitted in any form or by any means, electronic or mechanical, including photocopying, recording or by any information storage and retrieval system, without prior permission in writing from the publisher.

This book uses case studies to enforce the meaning behind its relevant chapter. Names have been omitted or changed to protect individual privacy.

Every effort has been made to trace (and seek permission for use of) the original source of material used within this book. Where the attempt has been unsuccessful, the publisher would be pleased to hear from the author/publisher to rectify any omission.

Cover design: Tess McCabe
Cover photography: Nick Tonzing
Editor: Sarah Fallon

ISBN: 9781922607805 (pbk)
ISBN: 9781922607812 (ebk)

A catalogue record for this book is available from the National Library of Australia.

Contents

Foreword ix
Introduction 1

January: Looking Within

Week One: Gratitude 3
Week Two: Humility 6
Week Three: Self-Awareness 10
Week Four: Respecting Differences 14

February: Getting it Done

Week One: Commitment 17
Week Two: Self-Motivation 20
Week Three: Leadership 23
Week Four: Being Energetic 26

March: Metacognition

Week One: Problem Solving 29
Week Two: Initiative 33
Week Three: Creativity and Imagination 36
Week Four: Decision Making 39

April: Family

Week One: Siblings 42
Week Two: Conflict with Parents 45
Week Three: Diverse Families 48
Week Four: Parental Pressure 51

May: Health and Wellbeing

Week One: Alcohol and Drugs 54
Week Two: Being Healthy 57
Week Three: Sleep 60
Week Four: Obesity and Eating Disorders 63

June: School and Beyond

Week One: Hating School 66
Week Two: Managing Peer Pressure 69
Week Three: Forming Relationships 72
Week Four: Homework and Time Management 75

July: Tough Times

Week One: Managing Bullying 78
Week Two: Coping with Loss 81
Week Three: Management of Failure 84
Week Four: Managing Anxiety 87

August: Looking Ahead

Week One: The Future of Our Planet 90
Week Two: Materialism 93
Week Three: Planning for the Future 96
Week Four: Independence 99

September: Accountability

Week One: Money 102
Week Two: Integrity and Honesty 105
Week Three: Community 109
Week Four: Responsibility 112

October: Modern Dilemmas

Week One: Taking Risks 115
Week Two: Respect 118
Week Three: Screens 121
Week Four: Dating and Sex 124

November: Awareness of Others

Week One: Listening 127
Week Two: Communication 131
Week Three: Negotiation 134
Week Four: Sense of Humour 137

December: Self-Management

Week One: Patience 140
Week Two: Staying Calm 143
Week Three: Stress Management 147
Week Four: Compassion and Kindness 150

Acknowledgements 153
About the Author 155

Foreword

Life is relational. We, as humans, are relational. It is how humans have and continue to survive and thrive. This important book leads you to a deeper understanding of this. As parents of teenagers we fully understand the complex relational matrix we have formed in our lifetime to date. We have also witnessed our children beginning to better recognise the relational imperatives necessary in their lives. The narratives given in each chapter of this book directly take the reader to life circumstances that illustrate the complexities faced by all as each navigates the inevitable and important relationships they will make or encounter. The teenage years are years where relationships are explored, and where peers as well as parents and other adults direct relational thinking. All parents want their offspring to lead content and constructive lives. All parents want their offspring to thrive. All know that mistakes will be made and that these will impact relationships and all parents want their offspring to be safe.

Read carefully each of the narratives given and think deeply about the underlying imperatives. Relationships are messy, they are dynamic, they challenge and it is within relationships that we develop our sense of being, our sense of purpose and our sense of worth.

A quality relationship has five defining elements. These are trust, forgiveness, integrity, hope and compassion. Trust is crucial for it provides the safety and security needed in all relationships. Forgiveness is "the" enabling element for it steers the path to healing relationships when mistakes and misjudgements are made. Forgiveness underpins the intention to "repair the relationship" when errors are made. We all err and every error impacts a relationship one way or another. We need to recognise this and understand the ongoing obligation to repair. Integrity really means that, within all relationships we try to do "the right thing". No one in any relationship is entitled to harm. The fourth element of a quality relationship is hope. Hope is the belief instilled which gives a sense of control critical to being positive and believing that one can achieve. Resilience is the restoration of hope. All parents want their offspring to be resilient in every sense but particularly in a relational sense. The fifth and final element is compassion. Compassion is "empathy actioned through care". Care is critical and life sustaining.

These five relational elements apply to each and every relationship and particularly apply to the relationship we have with ourselves. We need our teenagers to care relationally for themselves, to feel secure in themselves, to trust themselves. This then provides the positive basis for them to form quality relationships. Again this has been Illustrated with care within the narratives given and suggestions made in the chapters of this book.

Parents want their teenagers to form relationships on the basis of contribution, to be "givers" not "takers". To add value not to take value. No parent wants a teenager to be regarded by others as takers, users or someone who will exploit a relationship for benefit only. These people end up alone for others in the end grow tired of being used. Again, the advice given as you journey through this book is prescient for it directs you to steer your teenagers carefully into and through relationships that add value to their lives.

I encourage all to read with great care this important book. If your teenager forms quality relationships in life they will grow into a content and flourishing individual who will feel worthy and be judged so. We are defined not only by how we form relationships but also by how we behave in those relationships. Parents want the best for their offspring and this book will provide fodder for thought and action.

Read this book with purpose and share such with your teenager so that together you can chart the way forward.

John Hendry OAM
Educator, Speaker

Introduction

As my teenage children continue along their adolescent journey, I love seeing them face challenges that help them develop. Many of these encounters have been difficult, others not so. It is these challenges that continue to shape them. Some of these struggles aid the development of resilience, which will help them to push through when feeling nervous or anxious. Eventually, it will help them to become independent adults, able to face the many challenges that life will invariably throw at them. I want my children to become adults that can not only survive adulthood, but ultimately thrive. I'm sure many of us feel the same about our own children.

At the stage of writing this, Daisy is following her dreams and travelling through Europe on her own. Finn has just turned eighteen, gained his driving licence (and independence), and is completing his final year of secondary school. Monty is quickly heading towards sixteen and has found a passion for all things astronomical. I am so proud of my children and love watching them develop into amazing adults. I feel that I have done my best to help them. I am an extremely proud parent. But it has not always been easy.

Before I had children, I would often think about what type of parent I wanted to be. I watched how our friends and family would parent their children, often talking to my wife Sandi about all the great things they were doing. I would take the best ideas from all of them and dream of using them when I started my own family. After I changed careers and started teaching primary school children, I took some of these strategies into the classroom. I continually looked for ways of being a better teacher and also took things that I learned in the classroom back home. I was always questioning how I would, and later could, be a better parent. Sometimes I was successful, often I was not. I tried to learn from my mistakes, which I'm still making plenty of. I think that's the best that we can do as parents.

Teenagers often get a bad rap. They are frequently spoken poorly of. I think teenagers are amazing. British actor Kaya Scodelario was quoted as saying, "As a teenager, you're still discovering who you are, what your life is about, and who you want to be as a person. It's very intense."

It is in this book that I want to share many of the ideas that I've learned along my journey. Some of them will be great for your family, others will be terrible. You may agree with some of the things that I have learnt, you may disagree. But the most important thing for me is that you take the ideas that will work best for you and your teenagers. You know your children better than anyone in the world. Trust yourself and be comfortable to make mistakes. Some things you try in this book might be disastrous. Others may be successful. It doesn't really matter. Just spending time together is the best thing that you can do with your children. I also understand that this can be challenging for us at times as our lives can often be packed full. But I encourage you to start with just a few ideas from this book and notice what happens. Stopping what you are doing and spending some time together might be the change that you all need.

This book is organised into themes, one per month. Each theme has four topics, or executive skills, one per week. There is a total of 48 different executive skills in the book, one per chapter, that your teenager may need help with. Each chapter has a story that is linked to the topic. Some links may be clear, others may not. Sometimes you may not even see a link. You'll read teenage stories from ordinary, everyday people. There are people who grew up in all areas of the globe with a wide variety of experiences. Some are stories of success and happiness, others of sadness and struggle. Stories from people who have faced challenges that some of us can only imagine such as disabilities, drug addiction, eating disorders, death, and loss. All these stories are told by real people who have all experienced life as a teenager. They are stories from a moment of time in their lives. I really enjoyed interviewing everyone and listening to their stories, and I hope you enjoy reading them.

Have fun connecting with this book, as you connect with your teenagers.

In kindness,
Andy McNeilly

January: Looking Within

Week One
Gratitude

"He who knows he has enough is rich."

Lao Tzu

Gratitude could be described as the quality of being thankful. Being grateful for something may help us to become more connected with the present; not wishing for something from the future nor thinking about the past. There are many benefits to being grateful, such as improved mental health and increased happiness. Some say that showing gratitude can help decrease the chances of experiencing depression. It seems to me that one of the quests of being a human being is to be happy. Sometimes, when we just stop and 'smell the roses', we may become aware of the good things in our lives, even when we are experiencing other things that are not so good. Simply considering what we do have, rather than what we don't, may help us to simply be more appreciative. We may feel calmer and more at peace, which is a wonderful experience. We may even think how lucky we all are to be alive.

I am often thinking of the next thing and forgetting to experience the present. I will also think back to my past, focusing on my mistakes and thinking about how I could have done things better. I am rarely in the present. When I am, time seems to slow down. I find this when I am reading. I get lost in the words. Recently I was camping down the coast of the Great Ocean Road. I started reading and found myself totally immersed in the book. I was really enjoying the experience and didn't notice my surroundings. It was such a wonderful experience and I sometimes wonder why I don't read more often.

Choose one idea from this list to try at home together with your teen this week. Feel free to adapt or change it to suit your family. Maybe you have a different way to show gratitude as a family.

- ★ Write a letter or card to someone and thank them for something that they have done for you.

- ★ Imagine a family that lived in another country who have experienced a natural disaster or a war. Think about what they may be grateful for in their lives despite the hardship they have experienced.

- ★ What's the best thing that has happened to you today so far? What about this week? Discuss.

- ★ Talk about what you have learned recently that will help you in the future. Have you experienced something difficult and as a result learned something new?

- ★ Write a list of people in your life that you are grateful for. Share and compare lists with your family.

- ★ What are the best things about your family? Make a list and compare your list to other family members.

- ★ During dinner, talk about your meal and the things that you like about it.

- ★ What made you smile and laugh today? Chat with the family about these things. Notice others facial expressions as you share your experiences.

- ★ In silence, make a list of things that you are grateful for. Then compare them with each other. Are any things the same?

★ Think about a teacher or other adult who you are grateful to have met. Perhaps they helped you in some way or made a difference in your life. Consider giving them a call, sending them a text, or posting them a card.

Rhonda

My teenage years were both terrific and horrific. In my early adolescent years, my mum was mentally unable to take care of me due to the domestic violence she experienced, so I had to take care of myself. Domestic violence was a big issue in our house as my dad used to hit me too. I used to wander the streets of Melbourne at night on my own with no direction. During my first few years of high school, I was hardly there. At the end of year eight, my homeroom teacher connected with me every time I turned up to school, which was not very often. He would engage with me in conversation, but I was rude to him because I really didn't know what to say or how to act; I wasn't taught how to socialise and converse with others. My social skills were terrible. Mr O'Brien showed me that there were other possibilities that would enable me to live my life with kindness and acceptance, and he changed the course of my life. He helped me to feel that I had a choice to make changes that I did not see before.

> "Gratitude is the healthiest of all human emotions.
> The more you express gratitude for what you have, the more
> likely you will have even more to express gratitude for."
>
> Zig Ziglar

Week Two

Humility

"The sage puts himself last and becomes first."

Tao Te Ching

Humility could be linked to modesty. Someone who is humble may understand they do not have all the answers. They may have achieved some great things; however, they rarely talk or brag about them. When we are humble, we may have a realistic understanding of our strengths and also our weaknesses. Humility comes from the Latin word 'humilis', meaning low. It has been said that people who show humility may be able to better cope when feeling anxious. Humble leaders are often more effective as well as being better liked. They could also have a lower sense of entitlement, not feeling that they are owed anything. When we show humility, we may have better relationships with others as we are more able to accept people for who they are.

I notice that people at my workplace are a humble bunch of people. They are confident in their abilities when working with children and adults, and go about their business calmly and without much fuss. There are times when contracts need to be renewed and staff may need to reapply for their jobs, which can be stressful, particularly when competing against your work mates. I have been on interview panels and notice how challenging it can be for the interviewees to have to change their normal humble ways and start to talk about how good they are at their jobs. They need to sell themselves and their abilities, which can be challenging as it is something that they don't normally do.

Here are some ideas to help foster humility. Choose one that suits your teenager best and try it this week to see what you discover.

- ★ Choose someone to act as the waiter for everyone during dinner. Their job is to ensure everyone has everything that they need and even more. The waiter needs to go out of their way to make sure everyone is taken care of.

- ★ Perform some 'Random Acts of Kindness' for others during the week. Each night over dinner, discuss what happened and how you felt.

- ★ Do you know a famous person who has not let that fame 'go to their head'? What do you notice about them?

- ★ Talk about the people who do jobs that are often thankless and go unnoticed. Choose one of these people and thank them for doing the job that they do. You may like to tell them in person, or you could send them a note.

- ★ Play a card game or board game together. At the end, everyone including the winner, must be humble and thank each other for playing.

- ★ Go to the local park, lake, river, or beach and collect rubbish.

- ★ Talk about friends and family you know who are humble. What is it about them that makes them humble?

- ★ What mistakes have you made recently? How did you feel when you made the mistake and how do you feel now? Do you think it is important to admit making a mistake when you do? Discuss.

★ Some say that gratitude helps us to develop more humility. Make a list of all the things that you are grateful for.

★ Make two lists: one of all your good qualities and the second list of some of your limitations.

Rich

Bridgnorth in Shropshire was a beautiful market town to grow up in. The town was steeped in history with a castle and steam railway, and it had its fair share of ghost stories. As with many British towns in the nineties, there was a huge drinking culture. What would frequently happen on a Friday night, everyone would get kicked out of the pubs at 11pm and head to the chip shop or curry house where tensions would invariably rise, and fights would kick off. As a fifteen-year-old I looked up to the older guys and this is something that I aspired to be. Going to the pub was like a rite of passage. It was a community that I wanted to be a part of. One night I saw someone from school get completely beaten up, and I, as well as about 30 onlookers, felt powerless to help him. This shook me to my core. I vowed from that point that I never wanted to feel like that again. A short time later, I had a fascination for martial arts through some of the movies I watched. I wanted to learn how to protect myself and my family. I fell in love with the idea of aikido as a form of non-confrontational self-defense. I found a club and started training but I realised quickly that it generally takes about seven years to get a black belt. I moved to London and joined another club that had a very different style of aikido. To say I was mildly concerned was an understatement. These guys seemed to be knocking seven bells out of each other. Whilst every fibre in my body was telling me to walk out, I knew this was the place where I could get good. For the first three months, hardly anyone talked to me. I was the only white belt in a sea of brown and black belts. They eventually realised that I wasn't going away, so they took me under their wing, and I started training really hard. I still realised I was a long way off becoming a black belt. But I just kept turning up and continued to work hard. I read a book about an intensive aikido instructors course held in Tokyo, but you had to be a black belt to be accepted. I asked my instructor to write a letter of recommendation for me, and I ended up being accepted. Even though I spent a year getting my arse kicked, it galvanised my resolve not to get into fights. No one ever walks away from a fight being a winner. I had a new perspective on violence.

> "Humility is the solid foundation of all virtues."
> Confucius.

Week Three
Self-Awareness

"What is necessary to change a person is to change his awareness of himself."

Abraham Maslow

Self-awareness can be defined as being aware of one's own feelings and emotions. Some may say being self-aware is the key to emotional intelligence. Being self-aware can help us look within and understand how others may see us. It is a vital skill when working or interacting with others. I am passionate about many things and often get carried away during discussions. At times I've become excited and forgotten to listen to others. By becoming aware of this, I have noticed that I interrupt less and am beginning to listen more. Being self-aware can help guide us when deciding what to do and what not to do.

Working in schools, I notice that it takes time for our students to develop their self-awareness. They are usually totally oblivious of what is going on around them unless it impacts on them in some way. They can become immersed in what they are doing. I find this particularly so when they are engaged in some kind of play. They may only be concerned with what is going on with them and can find it challenging when others enter their space. As they grow older and transition through primary school, they learn more about themselves and begin to develop their self-awareness.

Following is a list of some ideas that may be useful for your teen to help teach self-awareness. Choose the one that suits your family best.

- ★ What do you really like to do in your spare time? Talk about why you think you like to do those things. How do you feel when you are engaged in this activity?

- ★ Is there anything that you avoid doing? Why do you think this is so? Discuss.

- ★ Write a list of all your strengths and your weaknesses. Share your list and discuss with others in the family.

- ★ Chinese philosopher Lao Tzu said, "To realize that you do not understand is a virtue; not to realize that you do not understand is a defect." What does this mean to you?

- ★ Talk about what makes you happy/sad/angry/frustrated/ecstatic, etc. If you are feeling an emotion that you don't like, what do you do to attempt to change that emotion?

- ★ Notice how you are feeling right now. Notice how your body feels. How are your shoulders? Your jaw? Your back? Your stomach? Your posture? Notice what happens if you change your posture? What happens if you stand up? Lie down? Roll into a ball?

- ★ Download a meditation app and use it to help you meditate. What did you notice about yourself? Try meditating a few times during the week. See if you notice any changes each time you meditate.

★ Canadian journalist and humanitarian Amanda Lindhout said, "With awareness comes responsibility and choice." What does this mean to you?

★ How do you think other people perceive you? What do you think they would say are your good and not so good characteristics?

★ Write down five strengths that you think you have. Then interview someone else and ask them to list five strengths that they think you have. Compare the lists.

John

Growing up in a very small town on the Murray River in Victoria in the 1960s, and being talented at sports as a teenager, gave me enormous prestige. Sports were important to me, and my parents wanted me to do well in school, so academic achievement was also essential. I played high level cricket, basketball and footy, which made people think highly of me. I was able to deal well with most things that were thrown at me in life as a teenager. I played first grade cricket and there were four teachers at my high school who were playing second grade, so I had to be careful how I managed myself when I was around them. I was relating to adults since I was fourteen as I played sport with them, so I was mature beyond my years without realising it. One day I was playing football for Northern Victoria against Carlton from the VFL, which was the highest level of footy in Australia at the time. There were more people watching the game than were in our town, as people came from all around the place to see us play. At three-quarter time, my younger brother came onto the ground as the coach was addressing us and told me that I was playing well. I rejected him at the time as I thought I was a man playing with men, but this was the last time I saw him alive. On his way home, he was hit by a drunk driver in a big car. He was rushed to hospital, and he died that night. As my twin brother had recently moved to a larger town in Central Victoria and my younger brother was not around anymore, I had to re-think my plans for my future. This was the first time that I had to consider others. The Carlton Football Club had offered to support me in my studies in Melbourne, but I wrote to them and told them that I could no longer take up their wonderful offer. I knew that my parents needed me as they were devastated by the death of my brother. I recognised that there was more to life than sport, and that the relationships in my life were far more important. I realised that as a teenager, the world did not revolve around me.

> "Emotional intelligence is your ability to recognize and understand emotions in yourself and others, and your ability to use this awareness to manage your behavior and relationships."
>
> Travis Bradberry

Week Four
Respecting Differences

"Strength lies in differences, not in similarities."

Stephen Covey

Every human being is different. We all look different, think differently and have different beliefs. Often, what you believe or what is important to you has been taught to you by your elders or your peers, or you may have learned them from the environment you have grown up in. Respecting other people for who they are and what they believe helps us to foster a more tolerant and caring community. It creates a more supportive and caring environment. Some personal benefits of respecting the differences of others can be learning more about other cultures and beliefs. This can even help to create friendships with people we may not have expected to. It might help us to be more empathetic or grateful.

I have travelled to many places in the world and the best part of all those experiences have been the people that I've met and the different cultures I have experienced. I've eaten in some amazing places and had some terrible experiences in restaurants. Once we met a Vietnamese-American in Dalat, who invited us out. He kindly took us to a restaurant that had some local Vietnamese specialties. When the food arrived, to our surprise, each dish was filled with a different piece of offal, the most confronting was an eyeball soup, with eyes rolling in the light broth, looking at us, waiting to be eaten. That was a very different meal. I can't say I respected it very much, but I did respect the experience which has left me with some strong memories and an excellent story to tell.

Select your favourite idea from the following list to try together with your teenager this week. Change or adapt your choice to suit your needs.

- ★ Listen to music from a different culture. How did the music compare to the music that you usually listen to?
- ★ Go to a religious event or ceremony and discuss what you noticed.
- ★ Find out about the indigenous people of your area and talk about what you discovered.
- ★ As a family, cook some food from a different culture that you haven't cooked before.
- ★ How are you different to others in your family? At school? Work? Your local community? Discuss.
- ★ Do you know what 'LGBTQIA+' stands for? Do you know anyone from this community?
- ★ Go out to dinner at a restaurant from a culture that you have not experienced before.
- ★ Make a list together of all the rude and mean names you can call someone who is different to you. Which names do you think are terrible? Are there any that are not so bad? Talk about how those people might feel if you called them some of those names.
- ★ Watch a foreign film or television show together.

- ★ Meet with someone from a different culture and ask them about the country they came from.

Damian

The one thing that stood out to me, growing up in the 80s, and now looking back, is that life was free and easy, with much less regulation. There was little political correctness. We called each other Wogs, Skips, Nips, Darkies, Chingas etc, and no one batted an eyelid. Even my sister's nickname was China. No one really cared. I was sometimes segregated, because I was half Chinese, but that was just life and we moved on, and bonded with the type of friends that didn't care about race. It was no big deal.

> "I look to a day when people will not be judged by the colour of their skin, but by the content of their character."
>
> Martin Luther King, Jr.

February: Getting it Done

Week One

Commitment

*"You always have two choices:
your commitment versus your fear."*

Sammy Davis, Jr.

Commitment could be defined as dedication and a guarantee that you will do something you set out to achieve, no matter what. Nothing will get in your way of achieving your goal, even when you face massive challenges or encounter setbacks that may stop many others. Being committed to a goal can help to keep you focused on the outcome. It can support you to work hard to achieve your goal and to realise success, even when you are faced with hurdles. Jill Koenig started her first company with only $100 at the age of 25 after overcoming a life of poverty. Five years later, she was a self-made millionaire. She was quoted as saying "Commitment is the glue that bonds you to your goals."

For some time, I dreamed of writing a book. I felt that I had it in me, but it was only a dream for a long time. At some stage, I decided to make it happen. I'm not sure what changed to make me commit, but I did. Once I made the commitment, things just started to happen. I made a plan and got into gear. I only did a little bit each night after work, but I usually kept my daily promise. If I didn't, I caught up the next night. I enrolled friends to help with the editing and feedback. I found a professional editor too. I found someone to publish the book and eventually I became an author. That seems like such a long time ago, and here I am doing it again. Sometimes when I am at my desk writing another book, I curse myself for the commitment I made, but I know that I will be happy once I complete it.

Following are some ideas to help foster commitment. Choose your favourite one to try together with your teen at home.

- ★ Set a goal to achieve by the end of the week or month. Plan how you will achieve your goal by breaking it down into small, achievable steps.

- ★ Make a list of some chores that everyone in the family will do to contribute to the running of the household. Check in after a month and talk about how you all went?

- ★ Discuss all the things that you are committed to in your life. Are you committed to some more than others? Why do you think this is? Discuss.

- ★ Complete a jigsaw puzzle within a time limit that you set for yourselves.

- ★ Choose a new skill, sport, or musical instrument you would like to learn. How will you achieve this? Do you need to create a plan to help you?

- ★ Build a house of cards. Decide how tall you would like to make it. Was this easy or difficult for you? Was your house too low or too high?

- ★ Think about something that you would really like to save for. Plan and set a date as to when you will achieve your goal.

- ★ Talk about someone you know who is committed. What do you notice about them? Do you know any other people who are committed? Discuss.

- ★ Plan to do something small every day for the rest of the year. It might be something very small but set up a checklist and mark it off every day when you do what you said you would do. Think about having someone as your coach who will help you achieve your goal.

- ★ Set a bedtime (or wake time) for everyone in the family for the week. Make sure everyone is in bed by the time they say they will be (or out of bed). Do you need to do anything to support each other?

Jutta

Going to school in Germany in the seventies was very authoritarian. It was the post-hippie era, and some of my teachers had a more relaxed approach, but this didn't work with me. The old-school teachers took the view that I was a bad student because I didn't perform academically. My parents weren't formally educated and didn't see things from different points of view. They saw things in black and white. I was kicked out of school when I was fourteen, so the shit hit the fan at home. During the summer break, my parents concocted a plan for me to work in their business and signed me up as an apprentice in textile design. This enabled me to legally leave school. I had to attend trade school and most of the time I put in very little effort. Trade school was all about the social connection. I was so unmotivated that my stepfather, who was also my boss, bribed me to pass the final exam because my grades were so bad. He said that he would buy me a set of bagpipes if I passed. This gave me some incentive and I did it and he bought them for me. Needless to say, due to my lack of commitment as a teenager, I never learnt to play them. But they hung on the wall in my bedroom successfully. Looking back on my teenage years and lack of commitment to my academics, and my hate of school as a child, I would never have thought that I would gain my PhD in linguistics.

> "You need to make a commitment, and once you make it, then life will give you some answers."
>
> Les Brown.

Week Two
Self-Motivation

"It always seems impossible until it's done."

Nelson Mandela

When we are motivated, we can complete projects or tasks without supervision or encouragement. We can stick to our word and complete something by a date, even when things become challenging. If we are motivated, we can get more done in less time. We may also find that we are way more efficient with our time. When we can see a goal in sight and we are motivated to achieve that goal, it seems that nothing can stop us getting there.

At times, some tasks seem so difficult to start. I can always find better things to do or very good reasons to procrastinate. When I am in this mood, I will often feel heavy and tired, which makes the task even more challenging. Some days, I just stop and decide not to start. When I consciously do make the decision to begin, I will just start. Often, I don't really know what to do, so I'll just do something. That something gives me the start. If I have an end goal and have already begun, then I'm away. The next thing to help me achieve my end goal is to break the larger tasks into smaller, achievable parts. I will work out how much I will do each day and calculate a date that I will have my project complete. And to help me, I'll sometimes get a friend to hold me accountable to my commitment. I'll let them know how much I will get done each week and keep them updated. All this helps me to get a large project complete.

If you feel motivated, choose one of the suggestions below. Pick the one that best suits your family to do this week to help them experience self-motivation. Perhaps you will choose not to do anything if you are unmotivated.

- ★ Set yourself a goal that you can achieve by the end of the week. How will you achieve your goal? Do you need to break it down into smaller steps? At the end of the week when you have reached your goal, discuss what you did to help you achieve success.

- ★ Choose a day where everyone wakes up early and goes for a walk together before breakfast. During breakfast, discuss how you felt and what motivated you to get up early.

- ★ What food do you really love that you find hard to resist if it is placed in front of you? Talk about how you might stop eating that food for a week. Do you think you could stop eating it for a month? Consider setting a food challenge for yourself.

- ★ Discuss what motivates you to achieve a goal. What do you do when the going gets tough? What can you do if you feel like giving up?

- ★ Talk about someone you know who is successful. How do you think they remained motivated to achieve their goals? Do you think they may have experienced a tough time and almost gave up?

- ★ Play some card or board games together. At the end, discuss the importance of winning the games you just played. How important was it to win? Did you really want to win? Or did you not really care? Why do so many people want to win? Discuss why you think some people are motivated to win while others don't seem to care.

- ★ Talk about some of your bad habits. Do you think that you could stop doing one of your bad habits? What do you need to put in place to ensure that you stick to your plan?

- ★ Plan a long walk or bike ride that you would like to do together and set a date. Complete your challenge no matter what gets in the way.

- ★ If you could have anything in your life, what would that be? Do you think this dream is possible? If so, how could you achieve it? Or is this dream impossible? Discuss.

- ★ Plan seven different things you will do together as a family for the week. Record them and make sure that you do everything you say you will do together.

Adam

As a 16-year-old, I was a reasonably successful athlete. I always wanted to win, but I don't know why. I could never sit still, and I don't know where my competitive nature came from. My old man had rheumatic fever, so he never played any sport and there weren't many opportunities for sport for women when my mum was younger. I played Representative Football and also won plenty of athletic awards, so you could say that everything was pretty cruisy. Then at thirteen, I had a knee injury and within six months, I beat the Australian champion in a 400m foot race. Four months later, the knee blew up again. I worked exceptionally hard and came back faster and better. Two years later, the knee was stuffed again. After this last surgery at 16, the orthopedic surgeon said in a wise, bedside manner, "If you don't stop, you will be in a wheelchair by the time you are 30." So, I stopped playing football, decreased my athletics obligations, and started playing Rugby.

"Once something is a passion, the motivation is there."
Michael Schumacher.

Week Three
Leadership

*"The role of a creative leader is not to have all the ideas;
it's to create a culture where everyone can have
ideas and feel that they're valued."*

Ken Robinson.

Many definitions of leadership can vary immensely. Some say it is the action of leading a group, some believe it is helping others achieve things they may not have thought possible for them. Others still may define leadership as overseeing a group of people, helping to get the best out of them. Leaders may be called 'The Boss'. But some leaders sit in the background and may appear not to be doing much. There are so many tips and advice on how to become an influential leader. So, what really defines leadership? Is it someone who leads by example? Or is a leader someone who inspires others? Looking at it literally, a leader is a person who is at the front. Or a leader could be someone who has a dream and gets others to believe in that dream, inspiring them to work together to achieve a common goal?

In my twenties I was fortunate enough to get a job in one of Australia's best restaurants, Stephanie's. The owner of the restaurant, Stephanie Alexander was a passionate and humble person who quietly led the team to provide a truly memorable dining experience for those who visited. She employed a team of people who were also passionate about food and the dining experience. Everyone who worked there were amazing professionals, giving their best to help the customers have an unforgettable evening. Stephanie was a great leader who made a huge impact on the Australian hospitality industry and continues to do so.

Choose one of the following ideas to try this week at home to help build leadership skills with your teenager.

- ★ Choose someone to organise a meal for the family that involves everyone doing something to help.

- ★ Play 'Follow the Leader'.

- ★ Someone is to plan an obstacle course in the garden or at the park and organise everyone to attempt to get to the end.

- ★ Choose someone to be the leader. They get to select a game to play and must convince everyone else why they should all play the game with them.

- ★ Without talking, select a leader. The leader must silently organise everyone to complete a task or play a game. At what point did someone start talking?

- ★ Think about something around the house that you would like to change, clean or tidy. One person is to get everyone organised to achieve the task together.

- ★ Go on a bike ride or walk together that is organised by one member of the family.

- ★ Play 'Guess the Leader'. Someone leaves the room, and a leader is chosen from the remaining group. The team follows the actions of the leader while the chosen person re-enters the room and guesses who the leader is.

- ★ Put names into a hat. Draw out a leader. The leader must assign everyone various jobs (including themselves) to clean the house. You may consider doing something else.

- ★ A leader of the family is chosen and needs to organise a family excursion, picnic, or activity to do together.

Linda

As a young teenager, I loved playing softball. I played every weekend and even played Rep softball, which meant I was representing my region. It was a high standard for our age. We were a chance to win the State Championships. At school, as our school sports were approaching, the teachers were selecting the teams for the inter-school sports. I assumed that I would easily make the first team. The teams were announced by displaying the team lists for the A and the B teams on the classroom window. As we all crowded around, one of my friends announced that I was in the B team. I was devastated. When I saw the list of who was in the team with me, I thought we would be totally crap. I went home and told my mum who was surprised. Mum spoke to Mr. Brown, who was the school softball coach when she saw him next and asked why I didn't make the A team. This was out of character for my Mum because she wasn't someone who would normally make a fuss about things. Mr. Brown explained that the reason I was selected for the team was due to my softball skills and that they needed someone who could lead and coach the team. When I realised that I was given this opportunity and that he trusted me, I threw myself into it and took it really seriously. I called extra training sessions. I looked at their strengths and helped them improve and they looked to me for leadership. We were successful in our division and won most of the games at the inter-school sports. I really got a kick from seeing the improvement from the girls in the team.

"The task of the leader is to get his people from where they are to where they have not been."

Henry A. Kissinger

Week Four
Being Energetic

"An energetic man will succeed where an indolent one would vegetate and inevitably perish."

Jules Verne.

Loads of energy and vitality – who wouldn't want a teenager that had more of this? Some people seem to have heaps more energy than others. But is this energy limited? Or is our child able to create energy from nothing, even when they are tired? Have you ever been tired and a good friend turns up at the door and somehow you are re-energised? Suddenly you become full of vitality. Can you imagine what it would be like if our kids could be enthusiastic and full of energy whenever they chose? If they were able to create energy out of nothing, what things could they achieve? Or perhaps they would become really annoying? Some of the benefits of our teenagers being energetic is that they would simply be able to get more stuff done. Others may want to be around them more as their energy can be contagious. They may even grunt less and complete some homework, or even help with tasks around the house – imagine that!

One of my work colleagues Mat told me about a friend of his called Dale. They both grew up in country Victoria and played football together. Dale had written a book called 'All Work No Play', made a Ted Talk, and started a podcast called Energetic Education. After reading his book, I contacted Dale and asked him if I could interview him for this book. He obliged, and we set up a Zoom. From the moment we started talking, I felt energised and enthusiastic. Dale is one of those people who seems to have more energy than most. After the interview, we decided to make a time to catch up in person. We haven't met up yet, and although I'm looking forward to meeting in person, I'm a little nervous about keeping up with Dale and all his energy.

Here are a few ideas you can try this week that may help your teenager to create more energy:

- ★ Get up early and see the sunrise together before cooking your favourite breakfast together.
- ★ Have a pillow fight with the family.
- ★ Go for a long bike ride or walk with each other.
- ★ Turn off the power without anyone knowing and pretend there is a blackout. Light some candles and see what happens.
- ★ Save some empty tissue boxes and use them as ice-skates. Play ice hockey or go ice skating inside. You may even consider some figure skating.
- ★ Go to the river, lake, or beach and skip stones in the water.
- ★ Have your teenager teach you their favourite game and play it together. It may even be a video game!
- ★ Blow up a balloon and play indoor tennis, soccer, volleyball, or any other sport you can think of.
- ★ Create a dance party in the loungeroom one night. Turn up the volume and have fun.
- ★ Have a loud argument about any silly topic you can think of.

Monty

Whenever it comes to something that I must put effort into, I find it hard to get started. Even if it's something I love, like astrophotography, I find it hard to set-up or even start. Because anything astronomical is at night, it means that I won't have a very good sleep and the next day I'll be tired. But the way I get my motivation is that I know that once I get started, I really enjoy what I am doing. The next day I'll be glad I did it because I really enjoy processing my images. When it comes to things like going to work, I never feel like it. But because it seems that I don't have a choice and it feels like I am forced to turn up, I don't need to be motivated. It also helps that I get paid so I can buy more astrophotography equipment.

> "In this very real world, good doesn't drive out evil. Evil doesn't drive out good. But the energetic displaces the passive."
>
> William Bernbach.

March: Metacognition

Week One
Problem Solving

*"Problem solving is hunting.
It is savage pleasure and we are born to it."*

Thomas Harris.

What shows up as a problem for one person may show up as an opportunity for another. A problem could be regarded as something that is unwelcome or unwanted and needs to be dealt with or overcome. Mathematical problems or conundrums may appear as a challenge to be solved. Problem solving can involve working through a series of steps to find a solution. And, once you have solved a problem, you might look back and wonder why you thought the problem was actually a problem in the first place. Can you imagine what it would be like if problems always showed up as opportunities?

In schools, I've noticed that problem solving often seems to be linked with mathematics. We teach our students to read the problem, highlight key words, and find out what the question is asking. Then the students can start to solve the problem. They use a range of different strategies, which are also taught. Sometimes the children come up with strategies of their own. The more challenging the problem, the more satisfied they are when they eventually find a solution. For me, this struggle is what we want our students to experience. This will help them as they face other challenges in their lives, not necessarily mathematically. The struggle can help to build their resilience.

Here are some fun activities to try together with your teen this week. Choose the one that best suits you both.

- ★ Work out what to have for dinner tonight without going shopping. Only use what you already have at home.
- ★ Find a new direction to travel to work/school/the shops. What did you discover? What different things would you see if you took this route?
- ★ Play 'Celebrity Heads' or 'Guess Who' together.
- ★ As a family, Google 'problem solving activities for teens' and work together to find solutions to the challenges you discover. You may like to Google 'conundrums' and see what you discover.
- ★ Imagine being stranded on a deserted island with no electricity. What would be the five things you would take with you? Talk about some of the things you would do to survive.
- ★ Talk about something that you usually do in your family. Then consider a change and say, "What if..." and complete the sentence. Consider trying out your 'what if'.
- ★ Get out a deck of cards and play a game you know together. Then, with your playing cards, learn a new game and play it as a family.
- ★ Stand next to each other with your hands beside you. At the same time, everyone reaches into the middle and holds hands. Together, you need

to untangle the knot of hands without breaking the chain. The idea is to finish in a linked circle.

- ★ Build a tower using only spaghetti and marshmallows or newspaper and sticky tape. How tall can you make it? Can you make a bridge with the same materials? How far can your bridge span?

- ★ Set a problem for someone else in the family to solve. Can anyone else solve your challenge?

Ted

I was keen for a surf, so I quickly picked up my mate, Sammy and headed down with high hopes, unaware of the disasters that would unfold. We arrived late in the afternoon at a little beachie that can only be accessed by driving through a private farm. We suited up quickly knowing that dusk was only around the corner, and in haste and excitement, I quickly threw my keys into a large bush thinking they would be safe. After a fun session we trudged back to the car in complete darkness, and this is where the problems started. Due to my youthful stupidity, I had failed to realise two important things; 1. Finding the keys in a bush thicker than Machado's afro was going to be hard and 2. Humans can see very little in the dark. Seeing as though I didn't have my night vision goggles with me, we started looking for the needle in the haystack in total darkness. After two hours of hopelessly looking in a bush that contained some nasty prickles, we decided our best bet was to walk to the road and flag down a car. Our plan was to get driven to a phone and call our best mate, Iguana who lived in the area to pick us up. It was going to be a long walk, but neither of us were keen on sleeping outside in our drenched wetties. About ten minutes into the journey, we hit the farm track, and it was then that we heard the disturbing sound of hooves trampling the ground. I didn't realise what it was until I could see the bulls' horns charging straight towards us. What we did next was something neither of us are proud of..... we squatted down, closed our eyes, and held hands. Maybe it was out of fear, confusion, or mutual love for each other, I can't explain. But what I can explain is that it worked because the bulls ran straight past us and faded into the darkness. With no further hesitation we bolted across the paddock, where we proceeded to slash our feet and step in cow shit. We finally reached the road and not one single car came by in three hours of walking. Eventually, we reached a little cottage where the owner was cool enough to let us call Iguana to come and pick us up.

"The best way to escape from a problem is to solve it."
Brendan Francis.

Week Two

Initiative

"Students must have initiative; they should not be mere imitators.
They must learn to think and act for themselves – and be free."

Cesar Chavez

Initiative can be defined as the ability to take action before others do. It might be having the ability to take that first step, to get the ball rolling. When we have initiative, we have the capacity to use our judgement to decide what to do without being told or asked. We may use other skills before being able to use our initiative. I love working with children and seeing them use their initiative. If a student has confidence with a particular skill or has a passion for something, it seems natural for them to take action and somehow know what to do next. They can often appear to be in a state of flow, being fully immersed in an activity. They can work independently and take actions to move their activity or project along to the next stage. I'm sure we can all think of a time when we have been in a state like this, and we naturally take the initiative without even thinking about it.

Years ago, when we bought our house, for some reason I thought it might be a cool idea to build a wood-fired pizza oven. I'm not sure where I came up with this idea, or even why. I had never laid a brick in my life. I went to YouTube and started my research. After many hours watching endless videos, I started the project. It took about five months to complete and after more than a decade, and hundreds of pizzas, the oven still stands in the back garden. Although it has many cracks in the dome, it is still working like it did when it was first built, maybe even better.

Here are some ideas or suggestions to help foster the skill of taking initiative. Or perhaps you would like to use your own initiative to come up with some ideas of your own.

- ★ Think of a card game or board game that you would like to play and get a group together to play it. What happened?
- ★ Some people say that others might not take the initiative for fear of being criticised or failing. Is this true for you? Discuss.
- ★ Organise a picnic or day trip somewhere with friends or family. Where will you go? What will you take? Who will you invite?
- ★ Look for an area in your life that could do with some organising or changing then get started. What did you notice once you started?
- ★ Set a goal to achieve this week. Perhaps set a different goal to achieve by the end of the month.
- ★ Make a list of different times when you used your initiative to get something started or to achieve a goal.
- ★ Think of an area in your life that isn't going as well as you would like then make a plan of the steps required to change it. Action your plan.
- ★ When you are asked to do something, do more than you were asked to do. What did you notice?
- ★ Next time you have an idea, speak up and share it with others. Were you nervous? Did they listen? What did they say?
- ★ Think of a new skill that you would like to learn. Research the skill and learn it. How did this make you feel?

James

When I was about sixteen, I attended a boarding school in Scarborough in the north of England. A few of us played the guitar and thought it would be a good idea to form a band. It was basically to give us something to do during the evenings as we were often bored. We weren't good friends at school, but we had music in common. There was a place to practise so we did so in the evenings and weekends. We started off playing covers but we all had different tastes in music which made it challenging at times. Eventually we started to write our own songs and entered a nationwide rock schools' competition. We sent in a tape of our recordings and surprisingly we became finalists, and each won a copy of a book called something like, 'How to Make it in the Music Industry'. This gave us the confidence to take our music further, so we sent some tapes to local pubs to try and get gigs, which we did. At the time, we earned a good amount of money for about an hour and a half of having fun and playing music. As we approached the end of school, we had some serious conversations about the future of our band. Weirdly, we chose to follow the steps of the book and try to follow our dreams. We booked into a professional recording studio and made a master tape and, as per the instructions in the book, we made multiple copies on a tape-to-tape recorder and sent them off to the addresses listed in the book. We then followed up with a phone call to all the recording studios, with no success except for one. I was put through to the A&R man who was responsible for talent in Polydor Records in Portobello Road, London. He invited us down for a meeting to discuss our future. We went in to these really flash studios and he put our master tape onto a fancy state of the art hi-fi. We listened to our tape together and I was so excited, dreaming about a future in the music industry. Unfortunately, we were gently let down. He mentioned that he might come and see us play live in Scarborough, even though he probably didn't know where it was. We all ended up choosing very practical careers and headed off to university.

> "Hold up a mirror and ask yourself what you are capable of doing, and what you really care about. Then take the initiative – don't wait for someone else to ask you to act."
>
> Sylvia Earle

Week Three
Creativity and Imagination

"The true sign of intelligence is not knowledge but imagination."
Albert Einstein

The Oxford Dictionary defines imagination as the act or power of forming a mental image of something not present to the senses or never before wholly perceived in reality. It can also be expressed as the ability to think of new and interesting ideas. Creativity could be seen as using your imagination to create something. To some, creativity is like innovation, imagination or originality. Perhaps creating a picture in the mind may be another simple way of defining imagination. It is amazing to me that young children can imagine anything, but as they grow older, some begin to lose that ability. What could be the benefits of an imagination that developed with age? It might improve our creative skills and possibly keep us younger. It may help us to transform dreams into reality and help us to dream big. A continually developing imagination may grow and feed our creativity. It may even help us to improve our memory and promote empathy.

When working with younger children, they will write some really creative stories. They can let their imaginations run wild. Some stories can be full of adventure and excitement, and once finished, they love reading them back to me. Often their handwriting is illegible, and I find it tricky to read. But they will know what they have written as they point to the words on the page and read to me. Sometimes if they read it to me the next day, there have been no changes in the written words, but what they read can be quite different.

Here is a list of ideas to help boost imagination and creative skills. Choose something to try at home together with your teen. You might prefer to create something different from the list.

- ★ Invent a short story and tell everyone. You can make the whole thing up or perhaps you could embellish something that you did as a family together.
- ★ Play 'Mr. Squiggle'. One person quickly draws a squiggle on a piece of paper and passes it along for the next person to complete the drawing.
- ★ Imagine you won the lottery. What would you do with the money? Discuss.
- ★ Make up some campfire or ghost stories to tell each other.
- ★ Cook something that you have never cooked before. Consider changing the recipe slightly. What did you discover? Discuss as you eat together.
- ★ Lie on the grass and look up at the clouds. Share what images you can see in the sky.
- ★ Rename the members of your family and your friends. Why did you choose these new names for them?
- ★ Play 'Charades' by acting out words and syllables in the title of a movie, a song, or a book.
- ★ Listen to some different radio stations and imagine what the band members look like. Where could they be playing their song? Can you imagine yourself somewhere else as you listen?
- ★ Rate your creativity skill on a level of 1 to 10. If you are below 10, discuss how you think you can learn to become more creative. Do the same with your imaginative skills.

Zoe

My teenage years were traumatic, so I felt that I had little capability to show any creativity or use my imagination. It started with the death of my grandfather, followed by the separation of my parents and a suicide attempt by my older brother. Just prior to all this, my Mum met her biological parents, and they told us that we were Aboriginal. It wasn't until a few years later that I was off the rails. School wasn't a safe place for me. I started smoking and I had no connection with my family – I felt very alone. I left school and fell pregnant at the age of about fourteen and had an abortion. My best friend passed away and there was at least one death in my friendship group every year for the next few years. Funerals became such a norm. At fifteen I moved out of home. I got my busking licence and learnt how to use the diablo. I'd busk in the city and earn enough money for the weekend. I'm not sure if I was being creative, but I had to do whatever it took to survive. I'd go to the Hari Krishna's and stack up the food and eat as much as I could. I started to hang out with the black fellas at the park in Fitzroy and this is when I started to feel like I belonged. I learnt about respecting elders and who my mob were. I finally found connection with community.

"Creativity involves breaking out of established patterns in order to look at things in a different way."

Edward de Bono

Week Four

Decision Making

"Good household decision-making often relies on thinking about your household like a firm."

Emily Oster

Think quick – make a choice now! We have all been in this situation many times before. When we are competent with something, like riding a bike, making a split-second decision can come naturally to us. However, when we are learning something new, or have not yet mastered a task or activity, making decisions may not come so quickly. It often requires more thought and analysis of the situation. Decision making can be thought of as the process of evaluating the alternatives and choosing the best option. Being able to decide quickly might help us save time and energy. However, sometimes decisions shouldn't be made too quickly. Standing back and looking at all the facts may prove to be critical when deciding the best course of action.

When riding my bicycle, I can quickly take all my past experiences and knowledge to safely escape tricky situations. Well, so far at least. It happens so quickly and effortlessly that it may appear to the observer that I was just lucky, like the time I was riding along in the dark and a rabbit crossed my path. It was either me or the rabbit. Luckily for me, it was the rabbit that came out second best, while I managed to stay on two wheels. On the other hand, I remember sailing in Oyster Bay on the east coast of Tasmania on a catamaran on a windy day. A wind gust blew and, being an inexperienced sailor, I was too slow to decide what to do and the boat capsized.

Carefully study this list together then quickly decide which one you and your teen would like to try this week.

- ★ Each person gets two different items. Take it in turns to put the first two items on the table. Everyone must choose one item by pointing to it as quickly as they can. Discuss why you chose that item.
- ★ Someone gets to think about two meals they might like to cook for the family during the week. They quickly call out their ideas and the first person who answers, gets to choose the meal.
- ★ Give someone two different characters to role play. They must choose one quickly then act out that character for a minute.
- ★ Watch a movie together. At the end, choose which character is your favourite and discuss why.
- ★ Someone says two different colours. The person sitting next to them must quickly choose one of the colours and say why it is the best. Repeat this game but change colours to animals, cities, sports teams, etc.
- ★ Get out two different board games. Have one person quickly choose which game to play.
- ★ Think about somewhere you would all like to go on the weekend. Between you all, decide where you will go.
- ★ Go for a bike ride or walk together. Each time you come to a junction, flip a coin to decide which way to go. See where you end up. You could also try this when you go for a drive.
- ★ Play a board game in pairs and each time it is your turn, work out what to do between the two of you.
- ★ Next time you are getting dressed on the weekend, let someone else choose what you wear.

Monica

At the age of sixteen, I was completing my final year of secondary school when I fell pregnant to my boyfriend. It was always my dream to finish school and study veterinary science. As it was a Catholic school, I would have been forced to leave if they had found out. Also, growing up in Colombia, abortion was illegal at the time. My boyfriend disappeared and it left me lost without any support. I was so scared to tell my mother. As I was having period-like cramps, I made an appointment to see the doctor. He sent me to the hospital to get an ultrasound. This is when my mother discovered my secret as she saw what was on the screen. I started to cry, and my mother did not know what to do. I remember seeing her face go pale and I just knew how scared she was. Everything was so tense. I really didn't know what to do. I thought that I wanted to have the baby, but I was really scared. My mother was a single parent working hard to get me through school. She worked so hard and did everything for me. We went to the park and my mother told me about her experience when she fell pregnant at a similar age. She wanted me to know that it would be a really hard thing to bring a child up on my own and I would be sacrificing my university. I would have to start working long hours for little money. She didn't want my life to be like hers, but she never forced me to decide. I had a couple of close friends I could talk to, but I knew that it was my choice. It was such a difficult time, but I decided to terminate the pregnancy.

"Inability to make decisions is one of the principal reasons executives fail. Deficiency in decision making ranks much higher than lack of specific knowledge or technical know-how as an indicator of leadership failure."

John C. Maxwell.

April: Family

Week One

Siblings

> "The greatest thing about siblings is you constantly have someone putting you in check; there's no room to get delusional about yourself."
>
> Erin Foster

The simplest definition of a sibling is a relative who shares at least one parent, whether biologically, or through adoption or marriage. Some siblings look very similar, others very different. Siblings can also have traits that are similar, or they may be completely different. It amazes me that children who grow up in a house with the same parents, and who have many similar experiences, can turn out to be so different.

My Mum and Dad had four children, including myself. After some time, my parents separated. Dad remarried and had three children with his new wife. Mum remarried a man who had two boys. Mum's second husband died after some time, while dad separated from his second wife and remarried again to his third wife who had three children. When it comes to my siblings, I really am not too sure how many I have. If anyone asks me, I really don't know how to give a simple answer. I wonder if my family is considered normal, weird, normally weird, or weirdly normal. I'm not sure if it really matters anyway. One thing I do know, we are all very different, while we also have many things in common.

Here are a few ideas to try that may get your teen thinking about their siblings. If they don't have any siblings they might like to do something with their cousins or even some friends.

- ★ Play some boardgames or card games with your siblings. Consider letting the youngest choose the first game.

- ★ Have a pillow fight or water fight with each other. You might want to do this outside, and you could wear bike helmets for extra safety.
- ★ Play 'Musical Chairs'. Think about who will control the music.
- ★ Put your feet into some empty tissue boxes and go skating around the house.
- ★ Play 'Pin the Tail on the Donkey' with your siblings. You may like to make your own version of this traditional game.
- ★ Sneak up and give a sibling a big hug for no reason at all. How did they feel? How did you feel?
- ★ Make some paper planes and have a competition to see which plane flies the greatest distance.
- ★ Go for a walk or bike ride together. You could plan the route before you leave, or flip a coin at each intersection to decide which way to go.
- ★ Do some 'Random Act of Kindness' for your siblings.
- ★ Plan a movie night or picnic with your siblings. Remember some drinks and snacks. You could even combine the two and watch an outdoor movie after the picnic.

Andrew

As I was just starting high school, I was riding my bike down the driveway. It was a steep driveway with a bend in it and we lived in a dead-end street so every time I exited our property and turned left on the road, I never really had to look out for traffic. Our street was always quiet. On this particular day, the next-door neighbour's truck was parked on the road. I hit my handlebars on the truck, came off and broke my arm in a couple of places. This was the start of me taking up tennis to strengthen my arm when it eventually came out of plaster. I took lessons and became fairly good. We lived close to the courts, so I'd play every night with my friend who lived in our street. I went on to play all the local tournaments and was a good player, but I never really won too many trophies. My two sisters who were younger than me, eventually found their way into tennis also. The eldest of them went on to become a really good player and won many tournaments. She was invited to the Institute of Sport in Canberra to train as a professional, but she declined. At the time, I couldn't understand why she didn't take up this opportunity, as I would have given anything to be in her shoes. My younger sister was different again. She just played tennis for the enjoyment. It was all about the fun; win, lose or draw. I remember asking my middle sister why she didn't go to Canberra. She said she knew that she'd miss her family too much and she felt she didn't have the physical attributes to compete on that level.

"Siblings are often very opposite."
Alycia Debnam-Carey

Week Two

Conflict with Parents

*"The first half of our lives are ruined by our parents
and the second half by our children."*

Clarence Darrow

The basic definition of a parent is someone's mother or father. Conflict might be thought of as a protracted disagreement or argument that is reasonably serious. Put them both together and we have conflict with parents. Some might think that living a longer time on Earth and experiencing a large range of different situations may give a parent some wisdom and the ability to provide counsel. But for some strange reason, a teenager will often think they have many more answers, if not all of them. What would a parent know? It can be easy to blame our teenager for any conflict. But, perhaps, it is us adults who create the battles. Wouldn't it be easier to just give in? On the other hand, we adults may need to hold our ground to teach our teen a valuable lesson or skill that will help them in their adulthood. When do we give in? When do we teach? Do we want an easy life right now or later on? Do we want our offspring to be independent and resilient adults?

Looking back, I remember the grief I used to give my mum. I was probably a typical teenager, but it seems like we were often arguing. I know Mum was always thinking of what was best for me, but I couldn't see that at the time. I wanted to stay out later than she would let me. I wanted to socialise and had little interest in study. I recall a time when we were both yelling at each other, and neither of us would budge. I have no idea what it was about, but it was most likely not very important. I was probably being extremely obnoxious and wouldn't stop. My mum gave me a big slap on the cheek, and we both fell silent. We were both stunned, and it was probably what needed to happen. I reckon it was probably deserved. It now seems funny to me as we have a great relationship with each other.

Following are some fun ideas to do with your teen. If they don't like any of them, perhaps you could force them to choose their favourite. Or you could just skip this chapter and move on. The choice is yours.

- ★ Make a Venn Diagram of jobs from around the house that may need doing. In one part are the jobs you hate. In the other part are jobs you like, and in the middle are all the jobs that are just okay.
- ★ Create a second Venn Diagram: jobs you like, jobs your teen likes and jobs you both like in the middle.
- ★ Have a pillow fight or slow-motion play fight together.
- ★ Comedian Rodney Dangerfield said, "When I was a kid my parents moved a lot, but I always found them." Discuss who you think wants to move first – parent or teen?
- ★ Make a list of all the things your teen does that you wish they wouldn't do. Now rate them from most annoying to least. How important are these things to you? Consider screwing up your list into a ball and putting it in the bin.
- ★ Have your teen create a similar list about you and have them repeat what you did. Discuss your experiences with each other.
- ★ Finally, both of you make a list of all the things each other does that you really like them doing.
- ★ Irish poet and playwright Oscar Wilde said, "Children begin by loving their parents; after a time they judge them; rarely, if ever, do they forgive them." Discuss what this means for your family and what stage your teen is at, if they are at any stage at all.
- ★ Have your teen choose a movie they'd like to see at the cinema and take them, no matter how much you don't want to go.
- ★ Consider taking a holiday together with just you and your teen. Have them plan the transport, accommodation, and meals.

Aung Say

At fourteen, I joined the Karenni Army, and we were taught to use guns to fight the Burmese Army. My father was angry with me, and he was also upset. He tried to convince me not to join by saying that if I joined, it would be a lifetime commitment. At the time I thought it was good as we had a uniform and we all thought we were older than we were. We weren't forced to join as it was voluntary. It was really hard, and after about a year, I realised that the army was not for me or my future, so I deserted and ran away early one morning. My father sent me to another town so they couldn't find me. I did some hard labour for a year before eventually returning home. I started farming until I later went to a refugee camp in Thailand where I stayed for eleven years.

"We never know the love of a parent till we become parents ourselves."

Henry Ward Beecher

Week Three
Diverse Families

'My parents split when I was 13. For a youngster, it's quite devastating. One minute you're all happy families, then everything changes.'

Vinnie Jones

Before we think of diverse or split families, we might want to think about what a normal family might be. Many definitions say that normal means to conform to a standard, or that it is usual or ordinary. But do we want to live in a usual or ordinary family, whatever that may be? Does a normal family have both parents living under the same roof? If so, does that mean that a split family is not normal? What about a family with a different structure to a mum and dad? Too many questions! One thing that has become more apparent to me as I get older, there is no such thing as normal. We may have similarities to other people, but we are all different. And so is every family. Every family is different. Split families, same sex parents, mum and dad families, step-parents, single parents, and so on. As American musician Thomas Rhett said, 'I'm a normal, horrible, screwed up human being like everyone else. I mean, I'm not a horrible person, but I'm just as screwed up as anybody.'

I remember observing a workshop being run for some year five students. The facilitator was doing an activity about similarities and differences in the group. The kids were standing in a circle, and he would ask them to step into the circle for different things. After some time, he asked them to step into the circle if their family was different. A few of them stepped in and he asked if anyone wanted to share what that was like for them. One girl put up her hand and said she loved her mixed up family with both parents who had re-partnered, as she had more people to love her.

Following is a list of ideas to help you and your teen to think about different families. Choose one to try this week together. Perhaps you could combine a couple and make something that is more suitable to your family.

- ★ Secretly draw a picture of what you consider to be a normal family. Compare your picture to others in the family.
- ★ Think about some people or families you think are not 'normal'. What makes them so special?
- ★ Together, make a list of all the weird or interesting things about your family.
- ★ Talk about what you all think makes a happy family and make a list. Are there any attributes on this list that you think your family have?
- ★ Princess Dianna said, 'Family is the most important thing in the world'. What do you all think about this? Discuss.
- ★ Talk about what you think a normal family is. Do you think your family is normal? Discuss.
- ★ Together, draw as many different types of family that you can think of using stick figures.
- ★ Play some board games or card games together as a family.
- ★ List all the great things about your family and then think about something that you would like your family to do differently.
- ★ Talk about all the families that are different to yours. Why are they different. Do you have anything in common with other families?

Pat

It was funny growing up and having older brothers and a sister, but I wasn't ever really sure if they were brothers and sisters. Every time someone would ask me how many siblings I had, I'd try and tell the truth and answer the question, but it never came across as straight forward. The reason for this is that my dad was married and had four kids before he met my mum. Together my parents had three kids, one of them being me. It felt like my half-siblings were more like cousins. When I was a teenager, they were adults in their twenties. I remember one of my half-brothers had a Mini Cooper and he came over on Christmas day. It was a pretty shitty car with a broken muffler, and it was low to the ground. It made the car feel faster than it was. Another half-brother took me and my brother for a hoon around the streets. He drove fast through the round-about and the police ended up pulling us over in front of our house. I can't remember much more, but I did think it was pretty cool at the time.

'I don't think anyone has a normal family.'

Edward Furlong

Week Four
Parental Pressure

*"Everything negative – pressure, challenges –
is all an opportunity for me to rise."*

Kobe Bryant

Parental pressure could be regarded as when parents try to persuade, coerce, or intimidate their teenagers into doing something. But why would they do this to someone they love so much? Could it be that these parents want a better life for their children? Or perhaps they are concerned by how their children may look or what others may think of them? Maybe they're embarrassed that their children did not behave as expected? These are questions that we may ponder.

My mum went to university, she was a teacher and she valued education. During my adolescent years, I had very little interest in education. I was interested in socialising with friends and planned to travel when I finished school. But Mum wanted me to attend university. Even though I had no idea of what I really wanted to pursue as a career, Mum thought it was important to continue my education. I don't really remember her putting any pressure on me, but I do remember that she was disappointed that I really didn't care about a future career. She just wanted what she thought was the best for me. Funny thing is, I eventually returned to education and became a teacher, just like Mum.

Following are some ideas to help your teen think about parental pressure. Consider pressuring your teen to do the one that you think is the best for them.

- ★ What do you think is the difference between peer pressure and parental pressure? Which one is more challenging for you to deal with?

★ Make a list of some things that your parents have pressured you to do. Put them in order from what your parents would consider the most important, to the least. Now put the list in an order that you think would be the most to least important.

★ Scottish historian and philosopher Thomas Carlyle said, "No pressure, no diamonds." What do you think this means when applied to parental pressure?

★ If your parents try to pressure you to do something that you don't want to do, try saying, "Thanks for the offer. I can see why you would want me to do this. But on this occasion, I am going to decline your offer." Notice what happens.

★ Do you think it is okay for parents to pressure you to do something they think is important? Do you think it is okay for you to pressure your parents? Discuss.

★ Make a list of all the different ways your parents have tried to get you to do something.

★ What could be some things that would be good for your parents to pressure you to do? Make a list and ask them to pressure you to do some of the things.

★ Next time your parents try to pressure you to do something, see what happens if you enthusiastically say, "No problems. I'll do it straight away."

★ Have you ever put pressure on your parents? What have you tried to get them to do?

★ Why do you think that parents pressure their children to do different things? Do any of these things really matter?

Sandi

I enjoyed playing tennis as a teenager. However, Dad was always on at me to practise. *You should be hitting against a brick wall*, he'd say. *You should practise more. You won't improve unless you practise*. The more he pushed, the more I didn't want to practise. The more he pressured me to improve my game, the more I didn't want to improve. I just wanted to play tennis because I enjoyed playing tennis. End of story. In the end I just stopped playing. Perhaps if he hadn't pressured me so much, I might have just kept playing because I enjoyed it.

"We feel pressure from every angle to meet expectations, but the pressure also pushes us in a positive way as well."

Momo Hirai

May: Health and Wellbeing

Week One

Alcohol and Drugs

"Kids are going to try drugs and alcohol; that's part of society."

Jamie Lee Curtis

Are drugs and alcohol bad? Or are they okay in moderation? Your idea of moderation may be different to mine. People will have different opinions and may argue about this until the cows come home. So, what you might consider okay for your family may be different to a friend or neighbour. And what is a drug anyway? Do you consider alcohol to be a drug? What about coffee? American writer William S. Burroughs said, "Our national drug is alcohol. We tend to regard the use of any other drug with special horror." Drugs and alcohol are often painted as bad. I've never seen alcohol or drugs jump off a table and head off into a person's body. I have seen people take them off a table and put them into their own bodies though. Drugs can help to cure diseases and improve lives. Alcohol can be used to help people relax and unwind after a stressful day or event. Does that make them good? I'm not sure what is right or wrong. It just seems as if everyone has their own opinions.

My friend and I thought it would be a great idea to try smoking when we were about ten years old. Our parents smoked and we thought it was cool. There were ads on TV promoting smoking and it painted a good image back then. We stole some money from one of our parents and went to the milk bar. I asked for a packet of cigarettes for my mum, the same brand that she smoked. The lady behind the counter somehow knew they were not for my mum, and offered another brand, saying they were a milder cigarette. I looked her in the eye, handed over the money and went off with my purchase. We went to a place near the train tracks and tried smoking, but I hated it. I was a terrible smoker and have not smoked since.

The following ideas might be useful to help discuss alcohol and drugs with your teen. You may wish to adjust or change any of these to suit your family best.

- ★ List as many drugs you can think of. Discuss if you all think they are good drugs, bad drugs, both, or you are undecided.
- ★ List as many alcoholic beverages you can think of. Discuss if you all think they are good, bad, both, or you are undecided.
- ★ What are the differences and similarities between beer, wine, and spirits?
- ★ Talk about the differences and similarities between drugs and alcohol.
- ★ If a parent gives you permission and feels it is safe and okay to do so, on a special occasion, you may like to try a different alcoholic beverage. Do you notice any changes in your body? Are there any that you like the taste of? Which ones do you dislike?
- ★ Bob Marley said, "Herb is the healing of a nation, alcohol is the destruction." What do you think he meant? What are your thoughts on this?
- ★ Go on YouTube and put the word 'drugs' into the search bar. Watch some videos together. Then look for videos on 'alcohol' to watch together.
- ★ Go for an excursion together to the local bottle shop. Look for things that you have never seen before and wonder what they might taste like. Consider asking the bottle shop attendant.
- ★ Research different types of alcohol. Can you find out what the base ingredient is? Research different types of drugs. What are they made of? What do they do to the body? How do you take them?
- ★ If you were to go to a party and were offered alcohol or drugs, but you didn't want them, how could you say "No" without losing face or feeling ashamed? Practise some of your ideas at home.

Jeff

From year seven or year eight, I was one of the only ones I knew who didn't drink or take drugs. As a result, my circle of friends evaporated – I had no friends. Probably the only reason that I had acquaintances during that time is that I was one of the better athletes in school. That didn't give me credibility, but I guess it gave me status. The summer between year nine and year ten I struggled. I didn't see a single person from my school because they tended to be drinking, partying, stealing their parent's cars and going for joyrides before they had their licences. I was too afraid of the consequences if my dad found out. There would have been absolute hell if he found out, and I also didn't want to let my parents down.

"Every form of addiction is bad, no matter whether the narcotic be alcohol or morphine or idealism."

Carl Jung

Week Two

Being Healthy

"To keep the body in good health is a duty... otherwise we shall not be able to keep our mind strong and clear."

Buddha

Being healthy seems to be very topical these days. Many of us are concerned with our body weight and image. Media seems to be telling us that we need to look a certain way. But how should we really look? How important is our body image? Is the look of our body connected to our health, both physical and mental? Being healthy may mean different things to different people. There is a load of research and data about the right foods to eat, and the correct amount and type of exercise we should all be doing. The question that I often ask myself about food and exercise is, "How does it make me feel?" If I feel good after eating it, then I'll eat more of it. If I don't, then I'll eat less of it. The same goes for exercise. I notice that after exercise, I feel more energised and focused. I can achieve more, even though I have spent energy, which seems strange to me.

I enjoy the feeling during and after exercise. I get up early most mornings and ride my bike along the roads or bike paths near the beach. Sometimes I play a quick nine holes of golf before work. On occasions I may be lucky enough to experience a beautiful sunrise. Exercise always energises me and helps me to sleep, as I am usually so tired at the end of the day.

Here are a few ideas to consider this week to help your teen with their health. Choose one or combine a couple to make it work best for your family.

- ★ Go for a brisk walk or run around the streets. Next try it along a river, at the beach or at the local park. Did you notice any difference?

- ★ Make a fresh salad and eat it slowly. Smell the food before you start eating. Notice the textures in your mouth. Listen to the sounds as you are eating.

- ★ How could you combine exercise with social media? Brainstorm some ideas and try some of them.

- ★ Go for a bike ride or walk and look at all the trees in your area. Talk about what you noticed?

- ★ Eat some chocolate or a sweet treat. Notice how long your enjoyment lasts. How does your body feel five minutes after eating it? What about ten minutes? Do you crave more?

- ★ Spend time on a device playing a game or communicating with friends. Notice how your body feels. Now do some exercise for 15-20 minutes. Does your body feel any different?

- ★ Make a list of 'Healthy Foods' and 'Sometimes Foods'.

- ★ If you were to do some exercise every day, what would be the minimum you could do to get you going? What exercise would you choose?

- ★ Cook a really healthy meal for the family. Include a healthy dessert.

- ★ Brainstorm all the unhealthy foods that you enjoy. Put them in order from your favourite to least favourite. Next, put them in order from most unhealthy to least unhealthy. Compare the two lists.

Mark

My parents had an investment property that was a building with some squash courts in it. It had a successful business that was going well and after some time, the lease was ready for renewal, but the owner was ready retire so he just walked out. So, my Mum took over the business as she wasn't working at the time. It was a busy place with tournaments and competitions, as it was a really popular sport in the seventies and eighties. My brother and I had never heard of squash, but we had a go at playing. We both had no idea what we were doing. Dave and I spent hours there each week, every night after school and weekends. We used to live on the courts as teenagers. We started playing junior competition, and then moved on to senior comp, and ended up playing men in the State League while we were still teenagers. At the time, some men hated being beaten by kids and would sometimes become frustrated. But I loved beating people much older than me. Exercise became important for me as I improved, but at the start squash was more about fun.

"The first wealth is health."

Ralph Waldo Emerson

Week Three

Sleep

"Sleep is the best meditation."

Dalai Lama

Sleep can be such a wonderful thing. It can be a time to escape, to recharge and to unwind. When deprived of sleep, it can be even more special for many of us. Over one hundred years ago, Former United States Senator Knute Nelson said, "In the midst of these hard times it is our good health and good sleep that are enjoyable." Perhaps this man was a visionary, as this seems so relevant to us in the twenty first century. There have been many reported benefits of getting a full night's sleep, such as an improved mood, a boost in our immune systems and better memory. Some say sleep can also increase our productivity, exercise performance and help us to build a stronger heart. All that being said, some say that too much sleep can be detrimental to our health. So, the big question we all may be wondering is how much sleep is the right amount? All this talk of sleep is making me tired!

When I was a teenager, I hated sleeping. I thought it was a waste of time. I'd rather be doing something, or socialising. Some of my friends would love a big sleep-in on the weekends and I couldn't understand why. I wanted to do something with them, but I couldn't as they were in bed, so I would easily become bored, and boredom is something that I still avoid. As an adult, I really enjoy the odd weekend sleep-in, particularly if I haven't planned much for the day. When camping, I may even have a nap in the afternoon. I now love my sleep.

Here is a list of things to consider when thinking of sleep. Choose the one that suits your family best.

★ What could you do when you can't get to sleep at night? Make a list of some crazy things you might try.

★ How many hours sleep do you think is right for you? What about other members of your family. Contact some relatives or friends and find out their thoughts. Compare what everyone thinks.

★ Talk about some of the funny dreams you have had. Can you remember any scary nightmares?

★ Google 'sleep tips' and make a list of the best ones for you. Consider trying some of them out.

★ When I can't get to sleep at night, I sometimes lie in bed and think, "Even though I can't get to sleep, at least I'm relaxing and will be well-rested tomorrow anyway." The funny thing that I've noticed is that I often fall asleep really quickly after that. Could this be something that works for you?

★ Make a list of any distractions in your room that may get in the way of your sleep. Can you remove some of them?

★ English novelist Anthony Burgess said, "Laugh and the world laughs with you, snore and you sleep alone." Make up your own sleep quote.

★ Research different dreams and what they mean. Are there any dreams that you often have? Do you think they mean something?

★ Is there any music that helps you fall asleep when you are having trouble? Consider making a playlist.

★ What about thinking about any sounds in nature that may help you fall asleep such as waves, rain, or a waterfall? Can you add to the list? Think about trying some of them.

Finn

As a teenager during lockdown, I started going to sleep a lot later than normal and sleeping less. On the weekends I would go to bed even later and end up missing the next day. It didn't really matter because there was nothing else to do.

This lack of a good sleep schedule really affected my mood and energy levels and I fell into bad habits with my sleeping. A while after lockdown had finished, I began to realise that going to bed earlier made me feel better and able to do more during the days. I had more energy and developed more motivation to work harder and do better at school. I still like to sleep in, but not too much because I don't want to miss the next day.

"Tired minds don't plan well. Sleep first, plan later."

Walter Reisch

Week Four
Obesity and Eating Disorders

"Yes, I talk about eating disorders and you know, excessive dieting and excessive exercising can be a sign of a mental illness... but when we talk about eating disorders... the issue is not the food or the exercise, the issue is a lack of healthy conception of self. That is the issue."

Sophie Gregoire Trudeau

We are often told that obesity is on the rise and that our current generation is the most overweight ever. With all the current research and information around, how could this be possible? Could it be because we have such busy lives and there is a huge availability of junk food and pre-cooked meals? Or perhaps it is that we spend so much time in our cars, doing less exercise than we have ever done before? Maybe it's the high rates of poor mental health that we are experiencing? Whatever the cause may be, society continues to view obesity as bad, when perhaps it should not be this way. In a world where discrimination is frowned upon, should people with weight challenges be victimised? Then there are other eating disorders like anorexia, bulimia and binge eating. Some may say that there is no singular cause to these problems. They could be linked to media and often unreal body image expectations. Other issues may be psychological factors such as poor self-esteem, depression, anxiety or negative body image. Once again, whatever the cause, these are issues that are not healthy for our teens.

I have always loved my food, and it was a pleasure to work with similar people in the hospitality industry for so many years. I love sharing food with friends and family. But it has taken me many years to not eat too much. My enjoyment of a meal would see me often going back for seconds, even though I knew I had eaten enough. My willpower was non-existent. It has taken me many years to be able to wait to let my food settle, before deciding if I wanted more. And I often find that I don't need any more after the wait.

This week choose one activity from the following list to do with your teen to help highlight the concerns with obesity and other eating disorders.

- ★ If someone had an eating disorder, what do you think could be some of the signs you might notice? Discuss.
- ★ Canadian scientist David Suzuki said, "We must pay greater attention to keeping our bodies and minds healthy and able to heal. Yet we are making it difficult for our defences to work. We allow things to be sold that should not be called food. Many have no nutritive value and lead to obesity, salt imbalance, and allergies." Make a list of some foods that you think he was talking about.
- ★ Draw or list what would your perfect meal look like.
- ★ Make a list of all the people you could talk to if you thought you had an eating disorder.
- ★ Imagine you had a friend who had a great sense of humour and could always laugh at themselves. What jokes might they say about their eating disorder if they developed one?
- ★ Make a list of all the eating disorders that you know. Rank them from the worst to least bad. Compare your list to others and explain why you put them in that order.
- ★ What do you think would be the most common eating disorder? Explain your thinking.
- ★ New Zealand prime minister Jacinda Ardern said, "Issues like obesity do, as you well know, have a knock-on effect to diabetes. So, we all are better off if we invest early in prevention." What do you think she might do to help prevent obesity?
- ★ Is there such a thing as a perfect body? What do you think a perfect body might look like? Compare your thoughts to somebody else's thoughts.

★ Some say that a major cause of eating disorders is low self-esteem. Do you agree with this? Could there be any other factors? Discuss.

Hannah

There isn't a whole lot that is funny about an eating disorder when you're in the thick of it. But apparently, they can be quite the cause of amusement post the fact. I remember sitting in a park with friends about a year after going through the worst period of my life. I sat watching as my friend bent over doubled in laughter. I had just answered her somewhat timid question about what I did at the rehab facility I had attended for my illness. I explained that we had spent a lot of time fixing our relationship with food, eating lunch and morning tea together, going out for lunch at a new venue once a week. Halfway through, she burst out laughing, exclaiming something along the lines of "that sounds pretty good to me"! I was incredibly offended at first, how dare she laugh at something as awful as that had been, didn't she know how hard those activities were for someone with an eating disorder? But after a pause, I had to admit that learning to eat lunch with friends did seem somewhat comical sitting on the other side of healing, and I joined in the laughing too.

"I realized that I had an eating disorder in which I controlled myself to a point that I would not let myself enjoy what I wanted to eat or eat what I needed to eat, all to stay a certain size."

Jeannie Mai

June: School and Beyond

Week One

Hating School

*"In school, you're taught a lesson and then given a test.
In life, you're given a test that teaches you a lesson."*

Tom Bodett

School can be defined as an institution designed to deliver education or training by teachers. Apparently, schools were originally invented about 400 years ago and the modern education system forged during the Industrial Revolution was designed to teach future factory workers to be punctual, docile, and agreeable, doing what their managers told them. What about schools from the twenty-first century? How have they changed over time? What things remain the same from 200 years ago? Whatever your school is like now, there are many adolescents who do not enjoy their experience there. There are many adults who also hated school for several reasons. Michelle Obama thinks attending school is vital. She was quoted as saying, "You have to stay in school. You have to. You have to go to college. You have to get your degree. Because that's the one thing people can't take away from you is your education. And it is worth the investment."

During secondary school, I had very little interest in study. School was all about friendships and socialising. I was always waiting for recess or lunch breaks, or the end of the day. Friday at 3.30 was one of my favourite times at school. Once the weekend started, I was in my happy place. I was even happy at the end of the day on Sunday. Monday morning, now that was a different story.

Following are some ideas to help you and your teen think about school and perhaps create the possibility of thinking differently about school. Choose the one that best fits your family.

- ★ Make a list of some of the teachers you have had along your schooling journey. Choose your favourite two or three. What was it about them that you liked? Consider sending one of them a card.

- ★ Make a Venn Diagram with someone else listing the different things you like about school. In the middle add the things you both like, in the outer parts add the things that only you like or only they like.

- ★ French author Victor Hugo said, "He who opens a school door, closes a prison." Discuss.

- ★ When you were young, did you play schools with your siblings or friends? What do you remember about this?

- ★ Are there any clubs or extra curricular activities that you could get involved in at your school? Perhaps you could consider creating a club if one does not exist.

- ★ Write down what you think are the worst three things about school? From your list, think about what you could do to make those three things just a little bit better.

- ★ What are some things that you are passionate about? Can you think of a way to combine one of your passions with school?

- ★ List some possibilities of what you would like to do in the future. Who at school can help you achieve your goals?

- ★ Write down all the best things about school. Now put them in order starting with your favourite. Do this again, but this time list the things you hate about school. Compare your lists.

- ★ Some people say that teenagers need a lot of sleep. Do you think that extra sleep might help you to enjoy school a little more? Record your sleep patterns over a week or two. What do you notice?

Rolf

I was sitting in my room, in the middle of year 12, at 3am, staring at the same empty piece of paper I'd been looking at for the last five hours. I was bored shitless, unmotivated, disinterested, disillusioned and aimless. Subsequently, I was well on my way to failing year 12. I didn't really know what to put it down to, maybe a teenage existential search for the meaning of life, maybe thinking the education system was a cookie cutter factory not interested in developing young brains, maybe quitting part-time work and sporting activities to focus on studying had left me floating. Maybe just being a lazy, poor student was the cause. Whatever it was, I was derailed. I stumbled on, spending a lot more nights not doing much study, right through to exams. In the end, I managed to pass, having taken enough interest, and doing enough work in a couple of art subjects to get through. Overall though the whole year was pretty much a write off and didn't get me into any of the tertiary courses I'd applied for. So, with having no idea what I wanted to do, completing year 12 had me headed primarily to the unemployment queue.

"What I remember most about high school are the memories I created with my friends."

J. J. Watt

Week Two
Managing Peer Pressure

"I think that no matter what you're doing as a teenager, you're going to be presented with peer pressure."

Sara Paxton

Peer pressure, or social pressure, can be thought of as others wanting to influence or change behaviours or attitudes. It could be defined as a group wanting you to adopt particular values or to take a certain action. We generally think of peer pressure as a negative thing, however it could be positive, such as friends strongly encouraging you not to make a poor behavioural choice. I have noticed that some teenagers who have higher levels of self-confidence are more able to deal with peer pressure. Other teens have very little interest in other's opinions of them, so they can sometimes seem oblivious to peer pressure. Travelling through the teenage years can be tricky for some, as they may be faced with more opportunities to deal with peer pressure. As risk taking behaviours may increase, we want our teens to be able to deal with pressure from their peers to help them stay safe and to make smart choices, whatever they may be.

When I gained my driving license as a teenager, I easily succumbed to peer pressure from my mates. We were in our final year of secondary school, and we all had cars. We'd go driving way too fast around the suburbs late at night. I felt the pressure to join in with my friends, and I put the pressure back on them too. We were all complicit. We were all lucky not be involved in any serious accidents, despite our cars not being very good or particularly roadworthy.

On our side back then was the lack of traffic on the roads late at night, and the scarcity of distractions teenagers face these days such as mobile phones. If we were born in the twenty first century and were to relive our past, it may have been a different story.

This week, choose something from the following list of ideas to help your teen consider peer pressure.

- ★ During dinner, have someone choose something from their meal that they would like to save and eat last. Everyone else's challenge is to pressure them to eat it first.
- ★ Ask someone to do something that they may not want to do. Their job is to make an excuse to leave to avoid doing what they were asked. Were they able to get out of it?
- ★ Have you ever been pressured by others at school to do something you didn't want to do? What happened? Discuss.
- ★ See if you can convince your teen to go outside and start singing in the street, or something else that they may find embarrassing. Can you get them to do it? Reverse roles and get them to try the same with you.
- ★ Make a series of requests of your teenager. Their job is to say 'No' like they really mean it. What did you notice? Now, ask them to complete some other tasks. Their job is to change the subject to avoid doing that task. What happened?
- ★ What kind of things might someone try to pressure you to do? Make a list then rank them from not so bad to really bad.
- ★ Give your teenager a glass of salty water and tell them it's a 'special drink', without telling them what it is. Everyone else must pressure them to drink it. What happened? Did they drink it? If so, what did you all have to do to make them drink it?
- ★ Who could you talk to if you gave in to peer pressure and did something you knew you shouldn't have done? Why would you choose them? Discuss.
- ★ Imagine you were invited to a party where you knew there was no alcohol allowed, but a few of your peers said they were going to sneak some in. What would you do? Discuss.

★ Make a list of your friends who you know would not try to pressure you to do something you didn't want to do. What do you think it is about these people that makes them that way?

Katie

In the late eighties I was about sixteen. I had a great group of friends that I enjoyed socialising with, going out, drinking, dancing, and having fun. Things started to change when the rave scene took hold in the UK which was exciting and a great temptation for lots of us. Some close friends went one way and got into the raving, taking ecstasy and acid. For me, that was not a road I wanted to travel down. This left me feeling a bit resentful as things changed. I carried on having fun, still socialising, but not with those old friends. I did feel like I lost them as we'd had so much fun together. I felt sad because I couldn't go out with them anymore and we drifted apart. It wasn't until some years later that we reconnected. The initial bond that we formed as early teenagers was still strong and still is to this day.

"Peer pressure is something everyone will face in school. You have to really go by what you think is the right thing to do. Turn to the friends you trust the most when you are put in a compromising situation. If your friends are making the wrong decision, then turn to your parents."

Madisen Beaty

Week Three
Forming Relationships

"The meeting of two personalities is like the contact of two chemical substances: if there is any reaction, both are transformed."

Carl Jung

There are many definitions for the word 'relationship' regarding human beings, and the one common thread is 'connection'. There are three main connections defined: through blood, through marriage or an emotional connection between people. But are these the only connections we have in a relationship? When first born, babies immediately start to form relationships with their parents. As they grow, they form relationships with other family members and members of the community. This seems to be a very natural part of being a human. So, why would this be such an important skill to develop further? Some would argue that this skill is vital for us to thrive in the various communities that we all live in. Many employers are looking for people who are skilled in this area. Another benefit of being able to form relationships with others could be that we are able to collaborate more effectively. It may also help us to simply enjoy being around others.

Ever since I was a teenager, I've always had a job when I wanted one. I worked delivering newspapers, helping the milkman, working in a pharmacy making deliveries on my bike and cleaning up in a butcher's shop. As I grew older, I started to work in restaurants where I developed my love of food and working with people. I believe that my ability to form relationships has been a part of helping me to gain these jobs.

This week, choose one of the following to try together with the family. Feel free to adjust one of them to make it more suitable for your teenager.

- ★ Ask someone what they are passionate about and listen to what they have to say without interrupting them. How long can you listen for without talking?

- ★ Phone a friend or relative and discuss a fond memory you have of them. Maybe tell them what you like about them. What did you notice?

- ★ Go for a walk down the street. Every time you pass someone, make eye contact, and give them a smile.

- ★ Do something extra at home by helping without being asked. Did someone notice what you did? Did they thank you? How did you feel if they didn't notice?

- ★ Plan a picnic and invite other families or friends along. Consider organising some games to play together.

- ★ Write a card for someone and tell them something that you really like about them. You may prefer to send them a text.

- ★ Tell someone that you love them and give them a big hug. What did you notice about them? How did you feel?

- ★ Next time you are at school or work, talk to someone who you don't normally talk to.

- ★ Organise a board game or card game afternoon with some friends. You could also plan a movie night together.

- ★ Go for a walk or bike ride with a person you don't know very well.

Dale

I grew up in country Victoria and life was all about sport and I played every sport under the sun. Sport was how I connected with my dad. At school I wasn't the best kid — I was crying out for attention as life was pretty tough for me at home and my parents worked really hard just to put food on the table. I was often in trouble in certain classes, and I butted heads with a lot of my teachers. I reckon I was a pretty shit kid. There were these two sport teachers who would always take time to ask me about my weekend and how my sport went. They would take time to make connections with me. They didn't just do it with me, they were building connections with all their students. They were taking time to listen and to build those relationships. They never had any trouble with their classes. They made me feel better about myself and changed my life as a lost teenager. They made me feel important and were two inspirational people that I hope I can live up to. This was such an important learning for me in my teens and I wish I had been better at understanding that as a kid.

"A good life depends on the strength of our relationships with family, friends, neighbours, colleagues and strangers."

David Lammy

Week Four

Homework and Time Management

"I am definitely going to take a course on time management... just as soon as I can work it into my schedule."

Louis E. Boone

Secondary school is a large part of life for a teenager. By the time they graduate, many of them have spent about a third of their life at school. Part of secondary school is learning to manage your time both at school and at home. Home brings the often-dreaded homework! Some teachers thought it would be a clever idea to call it 'home learning' instead, but I don't think too many kids were fooled. Homework seems to hold the stigma of a bad thing. But does it have to be this way? Many parents have spent countless hours trying to get kids to complete their homework. I often wonder why we do this for our kids. Perhaps, this could be an opportunity for them to develop independence? Or, to take responsibility for their own lives? At what age do we parents stop wasting energy on getting our kids to complete their homework? I think that I would rather spend the energy on something more productive than butting heads with my kids. How good could life be if we never worried about our kid's homework ever again?

Thinking of our children, we've never been bothered if they complete their homework or not. Early on we let them know that it is up to them. It is their life, and they need to take responsibility for their actions. If they don't do any of their homework, they are the ones who need to suffer any consequences. If they do and get good grades, they are the ones who gain the possible benefits such as entry into university if that is what they want. As parents, we have never experienced any stress or worry about our children's homework.

Here are a few ideas that may help your teen to think about their time management skills and homework. They could try one this week, or next week, or…

- ★ Is it more challenging for you to start your homework, or to stay on task when you have started it? Share your thoughts.
- ★ British politician Layla Moran said, "From a young age, pupils are put under immense amounts of pressure in high-stakes exams. Often, they're made to feel like their whole future depends on how they perform in these narrowly focussed tests." Do you agree with her? Discuss.
- ★ Consider forming a small study group to help complete homework together. Would this be helpful to you, or would it be more of a distraction?
- ★ Try splitting your homework into smaller chunks. Each time you complete a chunk, take a ten-minute break, and do something fun.
- ★ Watch a few YouTube clips on time management. Were any of them helpful? What small changes could you make to help with your time management skills?
- ★ What do you think would happen if you failed an exam or test? What about if you received a result at the end of the year that you were not happy with? Compare your thoughts with other members of the family.
- ★ Talk with your parent about the challenges and successes they had with homework when they were at school.
- ★ If you hate homework, suggest your parents complete it for you if you do some of the household chores that they hate. What did you both notice?
- ★ Who do you know who would not have an issue with homework. What do you think it is about that person that makes them that way? Do you think they like homework?
- ★ Some people think that regular breaks are needed when studying to improve focus and concentration. Make a list of different ways that you would like to take a break from homework or exam study.

Rob

With homework, I didn't feel any pressure at all. I didn't need any pressure. I revelled in doing homework and learning. When I was doing Latin in year ten, I leant all the verbs coming home on the tram. I was keen to learn that stuff. Sometimes I would stay up until one o'clock practicing algebra and studying physics. It wasn't really any effort. It was a joy to learn this stuff. There wasn't any pressure or any obligation. I just enjoyed it. I think that there was a mood in our family. My sister and my dad were not in that mood, but my brother and I were. My mother was not highly educated, and my father even less so. He left school when he was about 14, so he didn't even care. My mother was ambitious for me and my brother to go to university, which was unusual considering I grew up in a working class suburb of Melbourne in the mid-fifties. My mum never pushed me to do any homework. However, there was an expectation that I would do well, even though there was no pressure to do so.

"Home computers are being called upon to perform many new functions, including the consumption of homework formerly eaten by the dog."

Doug Larson

July: Tough Times

Week One

Managing Bullying

"If you've witnessed bullying or if you're being bullied, tell somebody you trust. Tell mom and dad. Tell your counsellors or your coaches. Tell your teachers. Tell an adult who you trust."

Stephanie McMahon

Many people believe that bullying has been going on forever. Some believe that it is a part of life and growing up. They may say that it makes us stronger and helps us to develop resilience. Be this true or not, does it make it right? American athlete Eddie Alvarez said that bullying in general is for cowards. But does this help us if we experience being bullied? Some people say that bullying has three main features: it involves the misuse of power in a relationship, it is ongoing and repeated, and it can cause harm. Bullying can be in person, and it can also be online. So, what can someone do if they experience bullying?

When I started high school, I distinctly remember locking my bicycle at the school bike racks. Two boys in the year above started to hassle me about something. They started to tease me and try to get under my skin. I looked at them with a blank expression then walked away. They tried it again the next day, and I did the same. Eventually they gave up and never bothered me again. I wonder if they tried to find another kid to pick on.

Following are some ideas to help prepare your teen if they were to experience bullying sometime in the future.

- ★ Make a list of things someone may bully another person about. Put them in order from bad to worst.

★ If someone was mean to you, what could you say to them to make them laugh? Have someone at home test them out on you. Could you make them laugh?

★ It has been said that there are four types of bullying — physical, psychological, verbal and cyberbullying. Can you give an example of each? Can you think of another type of bullying?

★ If you were a bully, what could you say to your victim? What could you do to them? Discuss.

★ Talk about what you think the differences are between being mean and bullying.

★ Make a big list of people who you could talk to if you experienced bullying.

★ Go online and find some resources or helplines that may assist you if you experience bullying.

★ Are there any other places apart from school where someone may experience bullying? Make a list and compare your list to others.

★ If someone you knew was being bullied, make a list of some things that you could do to help them. How creative can you all be?

★ Name three things that you could do to prevent yourself from being bullied? Can you think of any others?

Russ

In about year eight or nine, there were a few people who were the perpetrators of bullying against me. I remember one kid who made my life hell, and I didn't want to go to school. I was little and skinny back then. There was a lot of teasing, and I found it very frightening. I had a close group of mates that were with me at school and had been since I started in primary school, and I often played footy with them. They did their best to protect me, but they couldn't help when I was alone. The kids who bullied me were two years older, and the physicality of it was quite daunting. They picked on me due to my physical disability, as I was born without any hands and only one leg. As time progressed, the bullying eventually stopped. I felt the teachers weren't really any help to me at the time. It was my mates that were the most important support for me.

"It's very important to choose kindness and stop bullying."

Jacob Tremblay

Week Two

Coping with Loss

"Life is hard. Then you die. Then they throw dirt in your face. Then the worms eat you. Be grateful it happens in that order."

David Gerrold

We all know that one day we will all die. Or do we? Will there come a time when we are able to live forever? Or will someone create something so we never age? And what happens when we do die? Do we go to another place? This is something that many people have beliefs and opinions about, but there doesn't seem to be much proof either way. Does there need to be proof to make it real? So many questions that are so wonderful to ponder. When someone close to us dies, we may react in different ways. We could experience many different emotions. Experiencing death is something that most human beings will encounter in their lives. Even though we know that humans don't live on Earth forever, it doesn't make it any easier.

When I was younger, I recall finding out that my Pop had died. I felt an emptiness and that is all I remember. A few days later, the funeral approached, and I can't remember feeling any particular emotions, despite loving my Pop. He was such a character. He would play soccer with us and carry on like a silly kid, trying to make us laugh. During the funeral, it hit me. I started to cry. I became really upset as I knew that I would never see Pop again. I still think of him.

Here are some ideas to help you think about death and coping with loss. Consider the best one for your family, or create one of your own.

★ Roman Leader, Marcus Aurelius said, "It is not death that a man should fear, but he should fear never beginning to live." Who are some people you know who have experienced life to the full?

- ★ Google images of the *Grim Reaper*, a personification of death. Are there any other things that represent death to you?
- ★ Think about some people you know that are not alive anymore. What were some of their wonderful qualities? Can you think of any memorable stories about them?
- ★ If you were to die, how would you want to be remembered? If you had a tombstone, what would you want written on it?
- ★ If you were continuing to feel upset about the death of someone, who or where could you go to for help? Make a list.
- ★ What do you think would be the worst way to die? What about the best way to die? Discuss.
- ★ Scottish musician Annie Lennox was quoted as saying, "Dying is easy, it's living that scares me to death." What do you think she meant? Can you relate to this quote? Can you think of anyone else who may relate to it?
- ★ Some people say that grieving is a very individual process. Do you know anyone who has experienced loss or death? What did you notice about them? Discuss.
- ★ Do you think death could be considered funny in any way at all? Do you know any funny stories or jokes about death?
- ★ People react to death or grief differently and may experience sadness, shock, denial, anger, guilt, blame or relief. Can you think of any other emotions that people may experience?

Torben

I would spend a few days every school holiday on a personal development course as a teenager. I met a guy and spent lots of time with him, and we grew close. It was a genuine friendship and saying to another sixteen-year-old mate that I loved him, was not normal. It was a strong, trusting bond. When school was becoming more serious, I pulled away from the course to spend more time on my studies. We drifted apart but kept in contact from time to time. When

I was at uni, I got a call from my mum at one of the communal pay phones in the Halls of Residence. She let me know that he had taken his life and I felt really guilty because of the close friendship that we had. For a long time, I couldn't forgive myself or him for not telling me, as there was nothing that I wouldn't have done for him if I had known he was in this space. I knew he had been struggling, but I didn't know it was that bad. It was incredibly hard to deal with, so I drank a tremendous amount trying to deaden it all, and my studies went to absolute crap, but it hurt so much, and I didn't know how to deal with it. I felt a loss and there was a sadness that I couldn't shift. Looking back, I could see that I was depressed, and it wasn't until I was travelling in Spain a few years later that I experienced his presence in a cathedral, and I felt that he was with me. I am not religious by any means, but I somehow found through travel and soul-searching, that I was able to deal with his loss. I found forgiveness and finally knew that things were going to be alright.

"I intend to live forever, or die trying."

Groucho Marx

Week Three

Management of Failure

"I have not failed. I've just found 10,000 ways that won't work."

Thomas A. Edison

Failure could be defined as a lack of success. But what is success? Is success the achievement of an aim or purpose? So, if you have not achieved your aim or purpose yet, have you failed? And, if you have failed somewhere, have you succeeded in other areas? Why is it that some people who fail get down on themselves and can become stuck while others get up and persist, pushing towards their goal or creating new goals? Why do some people quickly learn from failure while others take no responsibility and even blame others? When we stand back and look at failure, all that really happens is we do some stuff, and it doesn't go to plan. That's it. Next, we start making up some stories about why things happened. We attach reasons to the things that happened. Maybe, it just happened that way? Nothing more, nothing less. Anyway, we seem to think that failure is a bad thing, and it shouldn't happen. To me, failure is just another part of life.

One student I was working with would often be brought to tears if he was unsuccessful at things. He seemed to lack the resilience that his peers had. We talked about what made him upset, but he had no idea why he started to cry. He could find no logic in it. I asked him to try to fail on purpose. I wondered what he might do. A few days later, I asked him how he was going, and he reported that his plan to fail wasn't working. I challenged him that he was a failure at failing.

He thought about this for a moment, then started to smile. For the next few weeks when I saw him in the yard, I asked him how his failing was going, and he replied with a smile on his face that he was a failure at failing.

When thinking of failure and managing our stuff-ups in life, consider attempting one of the following to do with your teen. Warning: you may fail if you don't choose the right one!

- ★ Bill Gates said, "It's fine to celebrate success but it is more important to heed the lessons of failure." Where have you failed, and what did you learn from that failure?
- ★ Some people say 'FAIL' stands for 'First Attempt in Learning'. What are your thoughts on this?
- ★ On YouTube, watch some funny failure videos together like 'Failarmy' or 'Fail Compilation'.
- ★ Japanese athlete Morihei Ueshiba said, "Failure is the key to success; each mistake teaches us something." List five mistakes that you have made recently and then think about what you could learn from those mistakes.
- ★ Failure builds resilience. Do you agree or disagree with this statement? Discuss.
- ★ As a group, make a list of all the benefits of failing. Discuss them as you continue to build your list.
- ★ British entrepreneur Richard Branson said, "Do not be embarrassed by your failures, learn from them and start again." What are some of your failures that have embarrassed you? What was the most embarrassing?
- ★ Google some images of 'failure' and discuss what you see and how you feel about those images.
- ★ Play a boardgame or card game together and make some mistakes along the way that benefit the opposition. What did you notice? Consider doing the same thing next time you are playing a sport or undertaking a recreational activity.

★ Michael Jordan was quoted as saying, "I can accept failure, everyone fails at something. But I can't accept not trying." When have you decided not to try something for fear of failure? Discuss.

Zdrav

When I was a teenager, my identity was formed around my sport and physical attributes. I always wanted to be the strongest, fastest, and best at what I did. Whenever I was suffering from an injury, I struggled. I felt lost at times. When I had setbacks and sport went away, I really didn't know what to do. I had to work it out on my own and I didn't have any resilience. I didn't have a growth mindset where it was okay to fail. Failure was thought of as a bad thing. I was angry with my parents as I felt they gave me no support. I had dreams of playing soccer for Australia. I remember being the team captain for Victoria playing against South Australia. We came into the changing rooms at half-time down 4-0 and I started to cry. Deep down I felt a pressure to perform, and I was expected to be a great sportsman rather than a good person. It took me a long time to get over this.

"It is impossible to live without failing at something, unless you live so cautiously that you might as well not have lived at all, in which case you have failed by default."

J. K. Rowling

Week Four
Managing Anxiety

"A lot of problems stem from a desire to avoid discomfort. For example, people who fear failure often avoid new challenges in an effort to keep anxiety at bay. Avoiding emotional discomfort, however, is usually a short-term solution that leads to long-term problems."

Amy Morin

Anxiety could be defined as stress or worry about something where the outcome is uncertain. But what outcome could be certain? Could stress, anxiety or worry be normal? If it is considered normal, is there a correct amount of it. Or how much is too much? All these questions are stressing me out. But maybe that's a good thing. It seems to me that everyone seems to be stressing out about stress these days. So many of us seem to be worrying about worry. And we are becoming anxious about anxiety. How would life be if we just accepted that it has stress, worry and anxiety. Or even better, if we celebrated it. There could be some positive benefits of these feelings. We might become more aware of our surroundings and perhaps take extra care if we felt anxious. Worry could help us to create a well-organised plan of attack when attempting challenging tasks. Can you imagine if we saw anxiety as a positive emotion that helps us?

In the early days of Daisy starting secondary school, she started to feel unwell in her stomach. We took her to the doctor who did some tests but could find nothing wrong. Daisy started to miss days of school, often claiming she felt unwell in her stomach. After some time, we took her back to the doctor. Following some conversations between us all, he turned to Daisy, looked her in the eye and told her that there was most likely nothing physically wrong and she just needed to go to school. She ended up going to a different school and things immediately changed. Later Daisy knew that she was worried about going to school as she didn't know if her good friend was going to be there or not. As an adult, Daisy still feels anxious at times, however this doesn't stop her from taking on new challenges.

This week you might like to select one of the following to help your teen to manage their anxiety. Please don't get too worried about choosing the correct one and feel free to make a mistake.

- ★ Make a list of some things that you worry about. Put them in order from most to least worrying. Compare your list to others.
- ★ American author Wayne Dyer was quoted as saying, "The truth is that there is no actual stress or anxiety in the world; it's your thoughts that create these false beliefs. You can't package stress, touch it, or see it. There are only people engaged in stressful thinking." What do you think about this quote?
- ★ What do you think the difference is between stress, worry and anxiety? Discuss. Which is better and which is worse? When you have finished talking, research what the experts say.
- ★ Think of your friends and family and wonder what they might worry or stress about. After you have done this, consider asking some of them and see if any of your guesses were correct.
- ★ Make a list of some symptoms that you might see in someone you think is experiencing anxiety.
- ★ Cartoonist Tom Wilson said, "I try not to worry about the future – so I take each day just one anxiety attack at a time." Does this quote make you laugh, worry or feel anxious?
- ★ Imagine if an anxiety disorder was called an anxiety quality. What could be good about having an anxiety quality? Make a list.
- ★ Do you think being in nature could help with anxiety? Talk about what you could do in nature that may help, then try out some of your ideas.
- ★ If you were feeling anxious and didn't know what to do, who are some people you trust that you could turn to?
- ★ Think about three or four totally different countries, including where you are from. What things might people from these countries worry about? Discuss.

Shiva

During my teenage years, I was growing up during the Iran/Iraq war. My older brother had to fight on the frontline. There were no phones or any way to access him, except for letters that we would get every now and then. I was constantly worried that something would happen to him. My mother would have to travel 800 kilometres on a very old and tired train full of soldiers to reach the frontline to see if her son was still alive. We were constantly worried for his life. As a teenager, I had my own worries too. I was a very sensitive person and withdrawn. I was often lost in my own thoughts. There were no distractions with things like good television or music, as all the money went to the war. I read lots and lots of books; lots of novels. I would imagine that I was one of the characters in the book. I used to draw portraits too and these were my hobbies. I would keep everything to myself. This is how I think that I dealt with myself. War made me very resilient. I could deal with so many problems when I later migrated to Malaysia and Australia. It made me stronger.

"We all have anxiety about things. We all have little insecurities, but eventually you have to face your fears if you want to be successful, and everybody has some fear of failure."

Nick Saban

August: Looking Ahead

Week One

The Future of Our Planet

"We need to think of the future and the planet we are going to leave to our children and their children."

Kofi Annan

Many of us have concerns for the future of our planet and our world. How will things change as we grow older? And how fast will they change? Many of us feel that change is accelerating, and we may feel uncertain of what the future may bring. Will we have a planet to live on as we grow older? Worrying about the future of our planet may cause stress or anxiety. It could be a cause of worry for us or our adolescent children. However, it may push us to act, to make a difference by creating a future that is filled with hope and possibility. Apart from some poor behaviour of our human race, there are also many wonderful things happening on our planet. Is the glass half-empty, or half-full?

At one stage in my life, we lived by a train track. We used to put rocks on the track as a train would approach and watch the train turn them to dust. One of our family friends came over one day with a can of spray paint. He was a few years older than me, and he encouraged me to help him graffiti on a wall next to the train line. In big capital letters, we wrote 'solar not nuclear'. I had absolutely no idea what that meant, but I still became involved. That was probably one of the only times I had any involvement with environmental action when I was young.

Following are a few ideas that may be useful to help your teen deal with any concerns about the future of our planet. Feel free to adapt them to suit your family.

★ Google, 'quotes about the future of our planet' and discuss them with the family. Start with your favourite and put them in order.

★ Make a list of all the bad things that are happening on Earth and another list with all the good things that are going on.

★ Do you think that humans will inhabit another planet one day? If you think this could be possible, talk about what things would be needed and how would it be done.

★ Make a list of inventions that have made a positive contribution to the world. Put them in order. Compare your list to others in the family.

★ Get out a map of the world and look at all the countries. Choose a country and talk about the wonderful things you know about it. If you know little about a country, find out about it, and share with others. Repeat.

★ Plant a tree in your garden or plant one for a friend in their garden. Find out what 'guerrilla gardening' is and consider doing some in your neighbourhood.

★ Make a list of people who have made positive contributions to humanity. What have they done? How has their contribution been helpful.

★ Vietnamese Buddhist Thich Mhat Hanh said, "We need enlightenment, not just individually but collectively, to save the planet. We need to awaken ourselves. We need to practice mindfulness if we want to have a future, if we want to save ourselves and the planet." Discuss your thoughts on this quote.

★ As a family, make a list of all the amazing things that are being done to combat Climate Change.

★ Go for a walk and take note of all the trees and gardens in your neighbourhood. Continue to the park or another natural open space and do the same. How many birds do you notice on your journey?

Daisy

For a while in my late teens, I thought about going vegetarian. I'm not even sure why, but I just didn't think I could give up eating chicken or salmon. I didn't think that I could live without them in my diet. I also thought that converting to vegetarian diet would have negative impacts on my health due to the lack of protein. One night we sat down as a family and watched a new documentary on Netflix called 'Seaspiracy' about the fishing industry across the world. This traumatised me in the best and worst way. Seeing the way that the fishing industry alone was rapidly contributing to climate change made me realise that I needed to do something. At this point, I knew I could give up seafood altogether and decided that I didn't need chicken either. For me, missing out on a few foods, despite how much I loved them, was absolutely worth it for me to play my part in reducing the impact on the environment.

"Our most basic common link is that we all inhabit this planet. We all breathe the same air. We all cherish our children's future. And we are all mortal."

John F. Kennedy

Week Two
Materialism

> "We live in a materialist world, and materialism appeals so strongly to humanity, no matter where."
>
> Wole Soyinka

Why is it that we live in such a materialistic society? Why do we value money and stuff with such high regard? We all know of people who continue to spend so much time in the pursuit of things, hoping that this will bring them happiness. Have you ever noticed that once we have reached our goal to get that thing that we have been hoping for, waiting for, dreaming of, that once we have it, the happiness it brings is short lived? We then look for the next thing. This is something that I have experienced, and continue to experience, even though I know it's something that doesn't really bring much long-term happiness or satisfaction. Materialism could be defined as the belief that money and possessions are very important things to strive for in life. Having money or possessions may bring some happiness, but at what cost? What is the true cost of chasing this dream? On the other hand, having money may enable us to give it away, helping others and easing their hardships or just simply helping to bring them joy. So, how do we find a balance?

I know that materialism and having all that stuff doesn't bring happiness, but that doesn't stop me wanting the next thing. Once I get the next thing, the experience of joy is often short lived, and I find myself repeating the pattern. I start to dream of what I want next. I'll go on YouTube and start researching. I'll talk to friends who already have the thing I want. I think of ways to get the money together. I know how bad consumerism can be, but I'll justify to myself that if I buy it second-hand, it is good for the environment. And so, the cycle continues.

Following are some ideas that may help your teen think about materialism. Pick one or two to try this week.

- ★ Make a list of some things that you would really like to buy soon then place them in order from most to least desired.
- ★ What is the most expensive thing that you would like if you could afford it? Compare your item with someone else in the family.
- ★ American businessman Laurance Rockefeller said, "Individually, people are finding that a simpler lifestyle provides greater satisfaction than relentless pursuit of materialism." Do you agree or disagree with him? Discuss.
- ★ Play 'Monopoly' together as a family. Are there any similar boardgames you could play?
- ★ Listen to the song 'Material Girl' by Madonna together. Turn up the volume and dance or find a karaoke version and sing to the music. What do you think of the lyrics?
- ★ Think of some things that you saved up for over a long time to get. Which things do you still use? Are there any things that you now think were a waste of money?
- ★ Think of some things that you have and really like that cost nothing, or very little. What is it about those things that brings you happiness?
- ★ Do you think it is possible to get to a stage in life where you have enough money, or do you think that you will always want more?
- ★ Can you think of anyone who you consider to be rich but still isn't happy with what they have? Do you think they are satisfied with their life? What do you think they could do to change their life?
- ★ Listen to 'Money, Money, Money' by Abba and take note of the words. What are your thoughts? Discuss.

Nick

Towards the end of primary school, I got my first job doing a paper round. This made my mum happy as it got me out of the house, and I started to learn about the value of money. I started to develop my independence and I had the financial capability to buy things that I wanted, such as accessories for my BMX bike. I worked wherever I possibly could through my teenage years, and whenever I could, including the holidays. I had a job in a theme park, one in a service station, and I was even a teenage Santa Claus at the Brunswick Shopping Centre then later at the Doncaster Shopping Centre. I was prepared to do anything. For me, working and being able to save defined me as a person. I've always loved being self-sufficient even as a teenager. I have never wanted to rely on other people to survive. I learnt to place a huge amount of value on the things that I purchased, and I always took care of them because I had to work hard to get them. I never really had a desire to get more than I needed. In the mid-eighties, I really wanted an Atari games console, but my parents weren't in the position to buy one as they were about two-hundred and fifty bucks, which was huge at the time. So, I worked really hard and saved up and got one. I also bought the games for it like River Raid, Pac Man and Star Wars. I don't know what happened to it, but I wish I had held onto it as it would be worth a fortune now! I was a mad collector of footy cards. I would buy and trade footy cards and would be relentless until I got the whole set. I even collected Kiss cards too as I was obsessed with the band at the time. It wasn't the idea of obtaining stuff for materialistic purposes, it was just the joy working hard to be able to afford the luxuries that I probably wouldn't have had.

"Materialism isn't the panacea that so many people think it is."

Pernell Roberts

Week Three

Planning for the Future

"There is nothing like a dream to create the future."

Victor Hugo

Past, present, future. The past has come and gone and no longer exists, except perhaps in our minds. The present is now, and only now. The present is the only time that exists. The future is yet to come. The word future comes from the Latin root *futūrus*, meaning "about to be". Does the future ever come? Or is it just a concept? Many of us worry for the future. We may ask ourselves if it will turn out alright or if we will be okay? As the future is unknown, we can be concerned that it may not work out the way we planned. But will the worrying make a difference? Can we be at peace living in the unknown of what our future may bring? We can make plans and set goals, but not all will turn out as we hope. Sounds a bit like life to me.

When I'm on holiday, I'm always planning the next two or three holidays. I love getting away and taking trips. For me, the joy of a holiday doesn't start when I finish work and begin the journey. It all starts when I begin to dream of the holiday. All the dreaming and planning is part of my vacation. It's the package deal for me.

To get you thinking about the future, choose one of the following to do together with your teenager.

- ★ Confucius said, 'If you think in terms of a year, plant a seed; if in terms of ten years, plant trees; if in terms of 100 years, teach the people." Talk to an older person and ask them what they would like to teach others.
- ★ What makes you nervous or worried about the future? Everyone is to write a list on their own before comparing lists with each other. Now do the same except this time think about what excites you about the future.
- ★ Choose a 'futuristic' movie to watch together.
- ★ American inventor Charles Kettering was quoted as saying, "My interest is in the future because I am going to spend the rest of my life there." Discuss your thoughts about this quote?
- ★ Make three lists of some things that you would like to achieve in one year, in five years and in ten years. Can you create some goals from these lists? How will you achieve some of these goals?
- ★ Sitting quietly on your own, draw a picture or create a 'word splash' of your future. What can you see? When complete, share your vision with everyone else.
- ★ Mattie Stepanek was an American author who published seven best-selling books on poetry before his death at the age of thirteen. He said, "Even though the future seems far away, it is actually beginning right now." What are some things that you have been putting off doing that you could start right now?
- ★ If you were to think about your future, what could be your purpose in life? If you were to define your purpose, could you start living this life immediately?
- ★ Talk to someone who is older than you and ask them what they wish they knew when they were your age? Would they do anything differently if they could see into the future?

★ American activist Ralph Abernathy said, "I don't know what the future may hold, but I know who holds the future" and American businessman Jack Welch was quoted as saying, "Control your own destiny or someone else will." Do you think that life is as simple as this or do you think other things come into play? Discuss.

Andy

When I was about three years old, my grandparents gave me a shitty little drum set. I loved playing on them, making lots of noise. Later on, my grandfather played Rock Around the Clock by Bill Haley and the Comets, and that was when I knew what I wanted in life. The music was amazing and all I could hear were the drums. From that day on, I was always on the drums. When I was fourteen, I got my first real gig with these old dudes who were about fifty and the band was called The Runaways. They were a cover band playing all the big hits from the fifties right through to the eighties. Music from the Beetles, Creedence, The Stones and so on. Mum would take me to rehearsals on Thursday night and we'd play gigs on the weekends, and I was rolling in the cash. I realised that I could make money playing rock 'n' roll. I started to focus on Australian bands like The Angels, Australian Crawl and Hoodoo Gurus which became my favourite band at the time. When I saw them up close, the drummer Mark Kingsmill was so powerful, he owned it. It was wild. I knew that this was what I wanted; to be on stage and doing what he was doing. Shortly after that gig, I packed my bags and my drums into my panel van and drove across the border to Melbourne to chase the elusive rock 'n' roll dream.

> "You can't connect the dots looking forward; you can only connect them looking backwards. So you have to trust that the dots will somehow connect in your future. You have to trust in something – your gut, destiny, life, karma, whatever. This approach has never let me down, and it has made all the difference in my life."
>
> Steve Jobs

Week Four

Independence

"The greatest gifts you can give your children are the roots of responsibility and the wings of independence."

Denis Waitley

Independence could be defined as having the ability to do something without help from others. It may be seen as the freedom of doing things on your own. Being independent can help us to increase our self-esteem and self-confidence. It may also make us more able to care for ourselves and others too. Being independent could help us to create our own destiny. However, being independent may mean that we sometimes don't ask for help from others. It may be limiting the possibilities in our relationships with others. Many believe that being independent can help us reduce our stress levels and increase our happiness.

Cycle touring is one of my passions, and I love getting away and being totally self-sufficient. In one of my panniers, I'll take my tent, sleeping mat, and sleeping bag. In another will be food, pots, pans, crockery, cutlery, and a small gas stove. I take a small amount of clothes, some spare parts, a pump, and lots of water. I love the freedom and independence of touring on a bicycle.

Choose something to try together from the following list to help your teen foster independence.

- ★ Play a quiz where each person takes turns to ask everyone else questions, like: What colour is the vacuum cleaner? Where is the hammer kept? How do you start the lawnmower? How do you put on a load of washing? What night do the bins go out? How do you use a bike pump?

- ★ Prepare and cook a healthy meal or snack for everyone else. Write a list of all the ingredients you need and help shop for them. Consider starting a book of your favourite recipes.

- ★ What is an important skill you need to learn that will help you become more independent? Ask someone to help you learn this new skill.

- ★ Plan and run a weekend activity, picnic, or family excursion. How did it go? Would you do anything differently next time? What did you learn?

- ★ What are the most important skills you need to learn before moving out of home? Rank them from most to least important to learn. Choose one of these skills and learn how to do it. How will you know when you have mastered this skill?

- ★ Create a resume and take it to some shops or businesses where you may like to work. See if you can get a job if you don't already have one.

- ★ Put on a load of washing, hang it out then bring it in and put it away when it is dry. Consider starting with something simple like a load of towels. You might even strip your bed, wash it all then remake your bed when the sheets are dry.

- ★ Tidy and reorganise your bedroom. Is there anything you don't need any more that you could donate to the op shop?

- ★ Think about some new skills that you would like to learn, then go to YouTube and see if you can find a video that will teach you this skill.

- ★ Help with the shopping by writing a list, going to the market and when you get home, help to put it all away.

Damien

Every Easter we would head off into the bush to a hut that Dad discovered with his mates. They didn't own the land, but they had an agreement with the owner that they could use the hut. It was about a three hour drive out of Hobart; two hours on normal roads which was followed by an hour on four-wheel drive tracks. While we were there, we wouldn't see anyone at all. It was really remote. The hut was insulated and lined with cardboard, but it was still draughty. It was very basic. We could hear the rats and mice under the floor, and nobody wanted to sleep near them on the bottom bunk. I was about thirteen and the Easter Bunny had hidden eggs all around the place. We'd find them in rabbit holes, snake holes and under the hut. I would wander off with my younger sister early in the day and we would share an air rifle and shoot at anything that moved without much success. We would try and set snares for the rabbits or wallabies, once again with no success. It was still exciting when a snare would be released. Sometimes there would be snow and it was really cold. We created adventures and played imaginary games, often returning home just before dark. It was so amazing that our parents would trust us with a gun, even though Dad had taught us how to use it. It taught us how to survive and problem solve. We were really resourceful, and we'd make stuff with anything we could find.

"Independence is happiness."

Susan B. Anthony.

September: Accountability

Week One
Money

"Money often costs too much."

Ralph Waldo Emerson

What is money? Some definitions say it is a medium of exchange. Money could be considered cash or credit. It might be banknotes and coins. Whatever money is, many of us seem to want more than we have. How much money is enough? How much money is not enough? Is there such a thing as too much money? Earning money may help our teenagers gain independence and learn the responsibilities of being a member of society. Spending it may help them to discover and experience the value of money. They may learn about what things are worth. By saving, they could learn patience and understand that some things are worth waiting for. They may also experience the financial cost of impatience. Another benefit of our teenagers earning money, is that they may start paying for more things themselves, therefore costing us less. What a win!

One thing that I've always loved spending my money on is holidays and travel. When younger, I'd often work two jobs and long hours. I was usually too tired to go out and party, so I'd save at a rapid rate for the holiday. I would do this for a few months, then the trip seemed even better, as I didn't have to work, often for long periods of time. The longest time I spent travelling without working was a nine-month trip. I travelled through Asia, across Russia on the Trans-Siberian Railway before eventually reaching Europe.

Following are some ideas that may help your teenager learn more about money. Change or adapt them to suit your family.

- ★ Play 'Monopoly' or any other money-based board game. You could try the card game 'Monopoly Deal' if you prefer to save some time.

- ★ Open a bank account and start to save one-third of everything you earn.

- ★ Find someone who you think may be in need and give them some money.

- ★ Play Poker or any other card games that require you to use poker chips. Consider using coins instead. Do you notice any difference between poker chips and money?

- ★ Place a pretend bet on a horserace or sports match. Did you win or lose? How did you feel as you watched?

- ★ Select a coin and save every one of those coins in a sealed jar or moneybox for a month. How much did you save? Use the money to do something fun together.

- ★ Take some money and spend it on something that seems really crazy to you. How did it make you feel? Did it feel like a waste of money?

- ★ Apply for a job somewhere in the local area.

- ★ Find out what someone in your family would really like to have and buy if for them, for no reason at all. Watch their face as you give it to them.

- ★ Hide some money in the house and the first person to find it gets to keep it.

Julio

I was really aware that Mum and Dad ran out of money at the end of the fortnight, and I used to worry about it. They never put it on us and didn't even talk about it in front of us. There were seven kids in our family. To go out to a restaurant was really special which we hardly ever did; maybe we went out twice each year. My parents always drove the shittest cars and I was so embarrassed. I vividly remember the time that I got a pair of Velcro white sneakers and acid wash baggy jeans in the middle of the eighties from K-Mart. I felt special. We didn't have much. We relied on sometimes getting a big garbage bag full of food from the bakery at the end of the day that was given to us for free and we all fought for the donuts or coffee scrolls. Sometimes we even got pies. We weren't poor growing up, but we were stretched at the end of the pay period. I still have a sense of comfort these days when I open the cupboard and it is full of food and the fridge has stuff for my family. It also makes me feel really happy that Mum and Dad are very comfortable now and they are so generous. They always share whatever they have.

"Never spend your money before you have earned it."

Thomas Jefferson

Week Two

Integrity and Honesty

*"The secret of life is honesty and fair dealing.
If you can fake that, you've got it made."*

Groucho Marx

Many dictionary definitions of integrity seem to say the same two things. Firstly, it is having the quality of honesty and secondly, having strong moral principles. Another definition I've heard is that integrity is simply keeping your word. Oprah Winfrey was quoted as saying 'real integrity is doing the right thing, knowing that nobody's going to know whether you did it or not'. Some of the benefits of being honest and having integrity may include authenticity and courage. Honest people can be seen to be more caring and may also attract other honest people into their lives. Honesty and integrity can help us to promote more trusting relationships and peace of mind and may also benefit our personal health. As Benjamin Franklin said, honesty is the best policy.

My brother was a particularly curious child who would often find himself in some kind of mischief. One day he was visiting a building site down the road from our house. He made friends with the builders, and I can imagine him chatting away and entertaining them. He would have probably helped them out in some small way too. In the middle of the day, the builders went off to get some lunch and left my brother there, telling him he could do whatever he liked. Taking this literally, he decided to break every window before heading home. The next morning there was a knock at the door and when one of my parents opened it up, they were looking at two police officers.

Choose one of the following ideas to try this week to help foster integrity and honesty in your family and with your teen.

- ★ Go for a walk and say you will be back by a certain time. Make sure you arrive home a little bit later than you said you would. Make a list of excuses as to why you were late. What is the difference between being on time, and being late with an excuse? Discuss.

- ★ Talk about integrity and honesty and what they mean. How are integrity and honesty similar? How do they differ?

- ★ Play 'Two Truths and a Lie'. Each person takes a turn at saying three things about themselves; two are true and one is a lie. Everyone else must guess which the lie is.

- ★ Have you ever found anything that was not yours and you really wanted to keep it? Did you keep it or try and find the owner? How did you feel if you found the owner? How did you feel if you kept the item?

- ★ Sneak something from the pantry or fridge that you are not normally allowed to eat. What did you notice and how did you feel? Did you eventually own up?

- ★ Should you always tell the truth? Is there a time when you should not tell someone the truth? Discuss.

- ★ Everyone is to hold something in their hand that cannot be seen. In turn, each person says what they are holding. Everyone else must guess if they are telling the truth or telling a lie.

- ★ What would you do if you found $10? What about $100? Or even $1000? Is there an amount that you should keep and an amount that you shouldn't keep?

- ★ Next time you are driving in the car together, tell everyone some things that you saw on the trip. Everyone else needs to guess if you are being honest or not.

★ Play a board or card game and try to cheat without being caught. What did you notice?

Ryder

My parents sent me to a secondary school they couldn't afford. I always felt the pressure because I knew about all the financial struggles at home. I was a year younger than my peers and felt that I had a bit of catching up to do. So, throughout years seven and eight, I wanted to prove my adulthood, or my masculinity. I started to gravitate to the boys who were the risk-taking ones. They were drinking and taking drugs. I wanted to feel more grown up than I actually was. We hung out one night and I smoked pot for the first time. It was terrifying and exciting at the same time. I bought a gram of weed and locked it in a little box that was in my room and went on school camp. When I returned, my mum would normally smother me in love. But this time, she had such a cold and angry look on her face. She asked quite a few times if I had anything to tell her, and each time I told her that I didn't. My mum was a hairdresser, and she had her salon at home. She told me that one of her clients who was a police officer kept leaving the salon before returning a few minutes later. She asked him what was going on, and he let her know that he had a new puppy that was in his car, and he wanted to keep checking that it was okay. In Mum's typical way, she let him know that the dog was welcome in the house, as our family were dog people. After a while, she went looking for the puppy and found it going nuts, scratching at a box upstairs in my room. She took the dog back downstairs and finished the haircut. As he was paying, Mum quizzed him about the puppy, and he admitted that it wasn't his dog. It was being trained to be a drug sniffer dog. Suddenly, it all clicked. I was in tears and felt humiliated. Although I had lied to my parents, they talked about the importance of honesty so that they could help me if I was ever in trouble. If they had locked down on me and been tyrannical, I reckon that I would have just kept on rebelling. But I didn't. I started to make smarter choices around drug use and eventually gave them up so I could concentrate on my studies. It wasn't until a few years later that I thought about what Mum had told me, and it didn't feel right as I don't remember her having any police officers as clients, so I confronted her. She admitted that while I was on camp, my brother was going through my room and he found the key to the box, opened it and found the gram. He didn't know what it was, but he was really upset and told Mum. She didn't want to tell me the truth because she thought it might ruin the relationship I had with my brother.

"With integrity, you have nothing to fear, since you have nothing to hide. With integrity, you will do the right thing, so you will have no guilt."

Zig Ziglar

Week Three
Community

"The greatness of a community is most accurately measured by the compassionate actions of its members."

Coretta Scott King

Community may be defined as a group of people that have something in common, such as living in the same area, a race of people, or even similar beliefs, hobbies, or pursuits. Community can be important to teenagers, as they find their place in our world. It may give them a sense of belonging to be part of their tribe or gang.

I remember when I was a teen, my main communities were bike riders, school mates and basketballers. I spent weekends adventuring around our local area cycling with friends. At school I would always be on the basketball court with my mates. I also spent hours with other school friends getting up to mischief of some kind. It was these groups that helped me to transition from child to adult, making many mistakes along the way, and sometimes learning from them.

Think about your community and what it might mean to you and your family then consider choosing one of the following to try this week. You may prefer to combine a few or even make up one of your own.

- ★ Have everyone list some of their *current* groups or gangs. Compare lists.
- ★ Now, compare your groups or gangs when you were a much younger. Are there any similarities? How are some of them different?

- ★ If you were to relocate to another community, where would you consider moving to? What is it about those communities that you think you would like?

- ★ American writer Anthony J. D'Angelo was quoted as saying, "Without a sense of caring, there can be no sense of community." What do you think about this quote? Discuss.

- ★ With a partner, talk about why you think it is important to be part of a community? Do you agree with everything that your partner said?

- ★ Consider one of the communities that you are part of and make a list of some things that you like about it? Is there something that you don't like and would like to change?

- ★ Do a 'Random Act of Kindness' for someone in your local community who you think would really benefit from it.

- ★ Talk about some of the communities that you think you could never belong to. What is it about those communities that you do not connect with?

- ★ Think about your local area and the communities that exist where you live. Are there any groups that you may consider becoming involved in that you had not considered before?

- ★ Is there a community that does not exist that you would like to bring into existence? What could you do to make this happen? Where could you start?

Jen

Through school as part of community service, I worked one afternoon every week in a nursing home. I walked there from school with some other students. We'd spend about three hours helping prepare meals. This was during the time of the AIDS epidemic and the cook who worked there said that you could get AIDS from kissing someone. I was quite shy as a teenager and would normally not speak up, but for some reason I challenged her. I felt justified and I didn't want to let this go. Now, as an adult, if I hear something that I don't agree with, I'll speak up, especially for the underdog, and particularly those who may not have a voice.

"The need for connection and community is primal, as fundamental as the need for air, water, and food."

Dean Ornish

Week Four
Responsibility

"You cannot escape the responsibility of tomorrow by evading it today."
Abraham Lincoln

Being responsible could be when we must deal with something or take care of someone. It may also be when we do the things we are supposed to do and accept the result of our actions. A responsibility could be defined as something that we are expected to do. And accepting responsibility might be thought of as taking the blame or being applauded for something we have done. Responsibility might help us to improve our organisational skills and help us with our commitments. As I get older, I seem to have more responsibilities. And with these responsibilities I make mistakes and also achieve goals, and I am better at accepting responsibility for both of those. So much to think about!

Being responsible for a class of children may seem like a daunting thing, but you soon don't really think about it. Early in my career I was teaching a year one class and the students from the adjoining room came to join my grade for a combined lesson. A while later, the assistant principal entered the room and asked if I was missing anyone. I shook my head, and she informed me that one of my students had left the school grounds and started to walk home. My heart sank. We jumped into a car and headed to the tennis courts, which were over a kilometre away. There was my student, talking to a kind lady who was gardening. The woman who was a retired teacher had phoned the school as she knew something wasn't right. From that day forward, you would see me regularly counting my students.

With your teen, think about doing one of the things from the following list to help learn about responsibility. Who will be responsible for choosing one this week?

- ★ As you have grown older, you may have been given responsibilities to help run the household. Make a list of some of the different tasks you have done over the years and rank them from most helpful to least. Compare your list to others.
- ★ When did you muck-up and take responsibly for your mistake? What did you do and how did you fix it up? Discuss.
- ★ Have you ever taken responsibility for a success in your life? What happened?
- ★ Write down some people you think are responsible. Why do you think they are this way? Do you know any irresponsible people?
- ★ Pleasure? Happiness? Responsibility? Canadian Clinical Psychologist Jordan Peterson said, "It's in responsibility that most people find the meaning that sustains them through life. It's not in happiness. It's not in impulsive pleasure." What do you think about this? Discuss.
- ★ Some people say that in order to take responsibility we need to stop blaming others and stop complaining. What are your thoughts on this? Is this easier to say than to do?
- ★ Open a bank account and put a set percentage of your savings and future earnings into the account. Do you think this would be a responsible thing to do?
- ★ Take on the responsibility of a task that someone else usually does at home. It could be vacuuming, cooking a meal every week, or regularly doing the washing.
- ★ Think of something challenging for you to do or learn and make a promise or commitment to complete this task by a certain time.
- ★ What does it mean to 'own your mistakes'? What do you usually do when you make a mistake? Do you sometimes blame others?

Andy

My father left mum as I was approaching the end of primary school. Suddenly, Mum had to take care of four young kids on her own. The family house was sold, and we moved across Melbourne to a suburb that was close to my mum's sister.

I felt that I had to grow up really quickly, and I did. There were four kids in our family: me, one sister and two brothers. We were really close in age. When we went away on holidays, I was always responsible for packing the car. I was often the one who read the map and gave Mum directions. I started to learn how to fix things around the house, not that I was very good. I started working to earn money at a young age as I felt that I needed to pay my own way with the things that I wanted to do. One of my jobs was working in a butcher shop, cleaning up at the end of the day. The boss gave me an offer that I could not refuse – he sold me two 1970 Renault 12s. One had a good body (which was bright orange), and the other had a good engine. Once I'd transported the cars home, I removed the good engine and thought it would be a good idea to rebuild it before putting it into the other car. I did this in my bedroom upstairs. I'm not sure how I got away with this, but I would certainly not let one of my children do this in our home! I started a new job over the summer in the local garage. I was able to get advice from the mechanics and all the parts I needed at wholesale price. Once the engine was rebuilt, it was transferred into the orange car and finally worked, thanks to the help of some friends. My bedroom was cleaned up and I now had the keys to my independence.

"Accept responsibility for your life. Know that it is you who will get you where you want to go, no one else.."

Les Brown

October: Modern Dilemmas

Week One

Taking Risks

*"The biggest risk is not taking any risk.
In a world that is changing really quickly, the only
strategy that is guaranteed to fail is not taking risks."*

Mark Zuckerberg

When searching for a definition of 'risky behaviour', many results added the words 'teenager' or 'adolescent'. Is that a connection that our society also makes? Is risky behaviour more prevalent in our youth? Are boys more likely to take risks than girls? How are their risk-taking behaviours similar and how are they different? So many questions! Risk taking seems to be part of us all as we grow up. Risk taking is often how we learn. But how do we manage our risky behaviour? What risks should our teenagers take, and which ones are to be avoided? This can be a challenging time for our youth and for us as parents. We want to encourage responsible risk taking from our teens, but which risks are actually responsible? Some say that risk takers can be more content and happier with their lives.

As a child, I was often up to mischief of some kind or another with my friends. We'd ride our bikes around the suburbs and spend the day out and about. We lived near a beach and there was a huge stormwater drain that fed into the bay. We had very poor lights on our handlebars, but that wouldn't stop us riding up the huge pipes underground. We'd end up at the main street and would call out from the drains in the gutters to the strangers walking up and down the footpaths. We were nervous at times, but it didn't stop us taking on these fun adventures.

Here are some ideas that may help your teens to learn to take risks while hopefully minimizing harm. Choose the one that best suits your family.

- ★ Blindfold someone and walk them around the house or outside while only issuing verbal instructions.
- ★ Play a board game or card game that encourages risk taking. Notice if your body changes when you are taking a risk.
- ★ What are some of the risks you have taken in your lives? Did any of these risks get you into trouble? Discuss.
- ★ Wear some clothes that you have not worn for a long time and go out in public. Maybe you could choose clothes for each other before you go out.
- ★ Cook something that you have never made before. The more challenging the better.
- ★ Tell someone a secret. How did you feel? What did you notice?
- ★ Some say that the biggest risk is to not take any risks. What do you think of this? Are there any risks that you have avoided?
- ★ Choose a day and say "Yes" to everything, not matter what.
- ★ Blindfold someone and have them taste different things from the kitchen. Watch their facial expressions. Consider taking a video of them to show them once you have finished.
- ★ Be impulsive and purchase something that you would not normally buy.

Sussi

Having to take risks during my teenage years was really important for me. I was exposed to taking risks through my parents, and sometimes even forced to take risks. These experiences formed who I am. After returning home to Sweden from a year overseas in San Francisco as an exchange student, I decided to head off to France to spend the summer as an au pair, to take care of a two-year old girl with cerebral palsy. I had studied a little bit of French, so I thought, 'Why not'. My friend's volleyball coach contacted the family in Paris via letter, they agreed, and that was the last I heard of it. We had agreed that I'd arrive sometime after school had finished. With only the family's address and not having contacted the family myself, I headed off on the bus.

"I prefer to be alive, so I'm cautious about taking risks."

Werner Herzog

Week Two

Respect

> "We don't need to share the same opinions as others, but we need to be respectful."
>
> Taylor Swift

Respect could be defined as admiration for someone due to their abilities, skills, achievements, or qualities. It can also be regarded as having due regard for the feelings, thoughts, rights, and opinions of others. Whichever way you define respect, it seems to be something that many of us find important. Respect often still seems to be important in our communities when considering age. It still appears important that we need to be respectful of someone who is older than us, or someone who holds an important position or title in society. It makes me think of the old saying, "Respect your elders." Many years ago, in its more literal sense, swearing or profanity was linked to a lack of respect. Some of us might say that this is still true. But aren't swear words just words? Do they really mean something or is the meaning made by the person who hears the words?

I remember swearing in front of my grandparents when I was younger. Everything seemed to be in slow-motion as I heard the word come out of my mouth. I wanted to push it back in, but I couldn't. Feeling embarrassed, I kept on talking, hoping that they hadn't heard me swear. I'm sure they did hear the word but they both just kept on listening to me, as I started to turn red. I can't even remember what the word was, but I do know that they would not have approved.

To think about respect and what it might mean to yourself and others, try one of the following this week with your teenager.

★ Each person participating is to think of three people they respect. Talk about what it is about them that you admire. Are there any qualities that you all agree show respect?

★ On a blank piece of paper, make a list of all the swear words you know. Next, cut them out and work together to order them from worst to best. Does 'best' mean the same to everyone in the group?

★ Irish singer-songwriter Bono was quoted as saying, "To be one, to be united is a great thing. But to respect the right to be different is maybe even greater." What do you think Bono meant by this? Discuss.

★ Think of different people who work in various occupations. Which of these do you highly respect? Are there any that you don't really respect? Why? Why not?

★ Years ago, two mottos about respect were, "Respect your elders" and "Children should be seen and not heard". What do you think about these two sayings?

★ What is the worst swear word that you know? Why do you think this word is so bad? Could you say it to a grandparent?

★ In cartoons or comics, swearing is often replaced by symbols. Think of some swear words and replace them with symbols. Give them to someone and see if they can guess what the words are.

★ Pakistani female education activist Malala Yousafzai said, "We should all consider each other as human beings, and we should respect each other." What do you think about this statement? Should you always respect others?

★ Think about a time when someone was rude to you. Why do you think they were rude? Do you think they could be excused for their rudeness?

★ What are some words that replace swear words? Make a list of the swear words and their replacements.

Kate

When I was a teenager in the fifties, I was washing the dishes with my sister Ruth, and I told her to "Shut up!". My Dad raced into the kitchen, and he could not believe that I would have said something so rude. I would never have thought to say "damn" or "bloody" or even "blast". I wouldn't have dared. We would never say those sorts of things. I can't even remember hearing the word "shit" or "fuck" in those days. One day I heard my Mum say, "blast" and even though I didn't know what it meant, I knew you could not use this – I think my dad was probably not around at the time.

"One of the most sincere forms of respect is actually listening to what another has to say."

Bryant H. McGill

Week Three
Screens

"Any excuse to get away from the computer screen is welcome."
Stefan Sagmeister

Any discussion of screen time and teenagers these days can evoke many strong opinions. It seems that everyone has something to say about screens and their teen, or teens in general. Too much time, addiction, bullying, anger, manipulation, and so on. However, many of our teens don't know life without devices. They have grown up with them and don't know any different. Perhaps we need to think about this before we give them a hard time. Besides, it was our generation who introduced screens to them! It seems to me that it isn't just our teens who spend too much time on devices. Many of us parents who have teens may model behaviour that we feel is unwanted with our children. Devices and many programs associated with them are designed to hook us all in. Millions of dollars have been spent to keep us engaged, always wanting more. As Steve Jobs said, "We made the buttons on the screen look so good you'll want to lick them." So, how do we best manage screen time for our teens, and also for ourselves?

Managing my own screen time has brought many challenges. I've tried many different tricks to minimise my screen time, as I know that I don't usually feel great after spending time on them. At home we avoid using screens while we eat dinner together every night. I never have my phone by my bed at night. Once I even made all the apps black and white. As I use my phone to tell the time, my home screen has no apps on it, so I must swipe before I can be tempted by those apps or red notification dots. Managing my screen usage is definitely something I find tricky.

Following are a few ideas that might help us all to better manage the time we spend on devices and screens. Try one or two or combine some to best fit your family.

- ★ As a family, discuss who you all think is on their screens the most and for how long. Install an app that measures your screen time and check your results at the end of the week. What did you discover?
- ★ Choose an evening during the week where you all commit to being off all devices and play some board games or card games together.
- ★ Sit together in a room and promise not to talk to each other. Send messages via your devices. Who can last the longest without talking?
- ★ LeAnn Rimes said, "Just because someone can sit behind a computer screen and have a different name and hide themselves, they feel like they can do anything to anyone." Discuss this quote together as a family.
- ★ Have you ever made a mistake when online? Share your online errors with each other.
- ★ Get out your device and share some of your favourite things to do on it with the family.
- ★ As a family watch some YouTube clips on 'screen addiction'.
- ★ Talk to a grandparent or older member of your community and ask for their opinion on screens and devices.
- ★ Watch a family movie together where your teen gets to choose the movie and the snacks. Decide if you want to put your devices away while you watch the movie.
- ★ Install an app or game that your teen loves and have them teach you how to use it.

Josh

My favourite screens are the television and the iPhone. On the TV I watch Netflix and some of my favourite shows are Peaky Blinders, Fast and Furious, S.W.A.T., and Harry Potter. I reckon I've watched all the Harry Potter movies over twenty times. On the iPhone I play games and text my mates. The games I really love are Call of Duty Mobile, Subway Surfers and Fortnight which I play on the laptop. When I'm on the screen, I get carried away. It's like reading a really engaging book, but ten times better. I get lost and time just drifts away. Being on the screen keeps me connected with my friends when I communicate online and when I get to school, we can talk about the same things, and I don't feel left out. Once I started playing Fortnight at about 10 o'clock and didn't finish until after five that day. I sort of feel like I'm a bit addicted, but I think I could give it up if I really wanted to. I remember going away for about a week and we didn't have any reception. When I got back, there were about 100 notifications which was my friends chatting and I missed it all. I felt annoyed that my mum wouldn't let me keep my phone for long enough to check all my messages. I also felt like I missed out on the chat with my mates.

"As parents, we have kids who reflect back to us our addiction to devices, and we have all sorts of worries about whether this is a healthy thing."

Franklin Foer.

Week Four

Dating and Sex

> "Some things are better than sex, and some are worse, but there's nothing exactly like it."
>
> W. C. Fields

Dating and sex can be the cause of some interesting conversations between parent and teen, if any conversations are had at all. Many people may avoid these vital conversations, preferring to keep away from any awkwardness. But avoiding them may provide the opportunity for even more awkward conversations in the future! Being aware of things that may happen when our teens start dating may give us the ability to help them. If they know what their peers, and kids a few years older than them are up to, it may prepare them so they are not hit with any surprises, and they may be able to avoid any unwanted situations. As they say, knowledge is power. Lots of education around this area these days comes online, and much of it is nothing like the real thing!

At high school, I went out with a girl in my year seven class. I'd spend some time on the weekends with her. A few years later when we were talking, she told me that she dumped me because I never took her hints. She would take me to somewhere private, like a local park, hoping that I would kiss her. I was so innocent back then that I had no idea. We both found it funny talking about the time when we went out together.

Here are a few ideas that may help your teen as they start to enter the weird and wonderful world of dating, and possibly sex. Choose something that works best for you all.

★ Talk to your teen about some of your dating experiences when you were younger. Were there any uncomfortable moments? Did you date someone you didn't like?

★ Do you remember your first date? Talk about it with your teen.

★ What does "No" mean? Does "No" ever mean "Maybe"? If so, when? Could "No" ever mean "Yes"? Discuss.

★ With your teenager, go on YouTube, search for 'sex stand-up comedy' and watch some videos for a laugh.

★ What was it like for you to fall in love for the first time? Discuss.

★ Watch some YouTube clips together on falling in love.

★ Watch 'Romeo and Juliet' together as a family. You may like to choose a different movie with a similar theme.

★ Mae West said, "Sex is emotion in motion." What do you think about this quote?

★ Go on to YouTube and search for 'first date comedy' and watch some things with your teenager.

★ Find a podcast about dating or sex to listen to it next time you are in the car together.

Josef

In year nine, which is the last year of compulsory school in the Swedish system, I was taking a class called 'Hemkunskap', which was 'Home Economics'. There was a girl in my class called Emma who was really pretty, and I had a crush on her. I wanted to ask her out, but I thought that she wouldn't be interested in someone like me. During the year, we exchanged some glances from time to time, but nothing more happened. We both moved on and had different partners throughout the remainder of school. Three years later, on Prom Night, we both started chatting. Emma told me that in year nine she had a crush on me, but she never dared to say anything. I told her that I also had a crush on her at the same time. We both thought it was funny, but also sad at the same time as we didn't dare act on our feelings.

"Love is like a virus. It can happen to anybody at any time."

Maya Angelou.

November: Awareness of Others

Week One

Listening

> "Listening is such a simple act. It requires us to be present, and that takes practice, but we don't have to do anything else. We don't have to advise, or coach, or sound wise. We just have to be willing to sit there and listen."
>
> Margaret J. Wheatley

People often confuse hearing and listening. When I was a kid, Mum would often ask if I was listening to her, and I would reply with a 'yes'. However, looking back I'm sure that, sometimes I was really listening to her and other times I just heard her. When researching different definitions of the word 'listening', the common themes seem to be paying attention or taking notice of something being said. The word 'listen' comes from the Old English 'hlysnan' which means 'to pay attention to'. Whereas hearing could be defined as noticing a sound, but not necessarily paying attention to it. Some of the benefits of developing our listening skills could include improving our problem solving skills, increased productivity and being able to create healthier interpersonal relationships. If we have well-developed listening skills, we may also find that we are able to save time and perhaps be more patient and respected. As Bryant H. McGill was quoted as saying, 'One of the most sincere forms of respect is actually listening to what another has to say.'

One time when I'd done the wrong thing, and Mum was telling me off. I can't remember what I had (or hadn't) done, but I was definitely in trouble. Mum couldn't believe it. She told me that I needed to change my ways, or else. I don't know what 'or else' meant, but I got what she was saying. She told me that

I needed to "pull my socks up". Without thinking, I leant down, took it literally, and pulled up my socks.

Read the following list aloud to your teen, let them listen to the choices, and then select their favourite to try this week to help improve their listening skills.

- ★ Make a telephone with some string and two tin cans. Use them to talk to a partner.

- ★ Give each other simple verbal instructions to follow. As everyone gets better, increase the number of instructions.

- ★ Go for a walk to the park or beach and sit quietly and listen to all the sounds. Write down what you hear then share your discoveries.

- ★ Play 'musical chairs' together. As the game progresses, turn the volume down lower and lower.

- ★ One person gets an item and describes it to others without showing them or saying what it is. Everyone needs to draw what is being described.

- ★ Write down some things that you can say to someone that cannot be correctly interpreted without another type of instruction. For example, without pointing, say "Look over there" or "Pass me that thing". Try reading the instructions and don't include the extra information.

- ★ Go outside and make a list of some possible sounds that you may hear in your house. Go back inside and see how many of the sounds that you actually can hear.

- ★ Is there a difference between listening and hearing? Do you agree with what was said earlier in this chapter?

- ★ Watch a movie together with the volume turned down as low as you can all manage.

- ★ Hide a phone somewhere in the house and then ring the number. Who can find the phone first? Try again, but this time turn the volume down lower. How low can you turn the volume down?

Graeme

My brother Brian and I had just bought our first car together. As I was born with no vision, I couldn't drive but I had saved some money. However, Brian had just got his licence and was desperate to drive. We were the perfect combination. The car was a blue Chrysler Galant, five years old, with a few miles on the clock, but we thought it was the best thing since sliced bread. We never missed an opportunity to take it for a spin. I had been asked by a social club in Wollongong to give a presentation to their afternoon meeting on people with disabilities. So, Brian and I decided to drive. For him, four or so hours behind the wheel of our little beauty was worth the tedium of listening to one of my presentations. I spoke about the importance of including people with disabilities in all aspects of society. I encouraged people to focus on the person, not the disability and to ask if assistance was needed rather than making assumptions about what we couldn't do. During question time I commented how critical it was to talk to the person themselves rather than about them. At the end of the meeting, we were invited to afternoon tea and were happy to partake of the excellent cakes and biscuits on offer. One of our hosts approached us and said to Brian, who was standing right next to me,

"Would Graeme prefer tea or coffee?"

I winced in disappointment, given the point of my presentation. However, 'coffee' was Brian's calm reply.

"Does he take milk?" she asked.

"Yes," Brian replied.

"And what about sugar?" she continued.

"Two sugars, please," was his calm response.

In contrast, my temperature was rising, steam was beginning to trickle from my ears, and I was planning the tongue-lashing he would receive during the drive home. His actions, I thought, had completely undermined my presentation.

"By the way," Brian said with a wry smile, as our host was about to leave with the coffee order, "Would you like me to drink it for him as well?"

Suitably chastened, she apologised to me, and my recompense was an excellent cup of coffee and an extra lamington. She had worked out the way to my heart.

"Most of the successful people I've known are the ones who do more listening than talking."

Bernard Baruch

Week Two
Communication

> "To effectively communicate, we must realize that we are all different in the way we perceive the world and use this understanding as a guide to our communication with others."
>
> Tony Robbins

Communication can come in various forms, including written, verbal, non-verbal and visual. Some experts in communication think there are even more types of communication. Often written communication needs to be carefully constructed to avoid any misunderstandings. Authors may need to consider the structure, clarity, and content of their writing. Verbal communicators may think about their tone and pitch as well as the content or the message. Often our moods or recent experiences can alter the intended message. Non-verbal communication, sometimes called body language, can be used both intentionally and non-intentionally. This form of communication can include facial expressions, posture, gestures, physical touch, and eye contact. Finally, visual communication has become extremely popular in recent times since the introduction of the internet and social media. Communication researchers have suggested that many more moods and intentions are transferred non-verbally than verbally, written or visual. Often, non-verbal messages can complement spoken language and it can be a wonderful substitute for words, particularly if there is noise or distance to hinder communication. As the well-known proverb states: actions speak louder than words.

In the school yard, kids get up to all kinds of things. I love watching all the creativity, games, and fun they often have. Sometimes they'll push the boundaries and do things they shouldn't. Sometimes they get away with it, other times they get caught. Often, I'll catch a student doing the wrong thing and I might look at them and give a subtle shake of the head. They will most often stop doing what they were doing or were about to do. I'll then give them a wink or a thumbs-up as a thanks, and head off.

To help think about the various methods of communication, choose the best activity below to suit your teenager and family.

- ★ During dinner, have a conversation around the table without saying anything. What different forms of communication did you use?
- ★ Everyone writes down an instruction on a piece of paper so that nobody else can see it. Pass the instruction to someone else. The person who has received the instruction must get someone else to do what it says on the paper without talking.
- ★ Get some scrap paper and write some short text messages or emails that may have more than one meaning.
- ★ Play 'Charades' together.
- ★ Make four headings of different forms of communication: written, verbal, non-verbal, and visual. Create a list under each heading of the different ways you can communicate in this area. For example, under written you could send a text, write a letter, leave a note, and so forth.
- ★ Play a board game or card game together without talking. Consider only communicating with each other via text or written notes.
- ★ Make three requests of someone in your family in one go. The person must first listen to all three requests before choosing one to accept, declining another, and making a counteroffer for the third one.
- ★ Think of some non-verbal communication facial expressions or hand signals. Try them on someone else and see if they get your meaning.
- ★ Go to the beach and write some messages in the sand for someone else to see. Consider using some visuals to replace some of your words.
- ★ Go to some social media platforms together and look for some forms of visual communication. Can you find messages that are clear and others that are not so clear?

Gail

My mother died when I was four and we were living in England, but I was sixteen before I actually knew how she died. I grew up knowing that she had died, but never really questioned what happened. I never thought to ask how or why she died. I remember her being in hospital and visiting while she had a blood transfusion. I was fascinated watching the blood go into her veins. In my mind, her dying was a continuation of her being unwell. When I was sixteen years old, now living in South Africa, my life insurance matured, and I was taking out a new insurance. I had to complete some forms with my father, and state how my mother had died. My father wrote down that she died of gas poisoning. I later asked my father for more details about her death. He became upset as he thought that I already knew that my mother had committed suicide. My father assumed that his mother, my grandmother, had told me. Meanwhile, my grandmother thought that my father had told me. Obviously, there was a breakdown in communication between my father and his mother. My father became upset again as he re-lived her death. As a teenager, I was thinking selfishly that my mother may have passed on her 'mad genes' to me. I was also angry with her because I thought that she obviously didn't love me enough to want to stay alive. It wasn't until I did nursing that I realised what depression can do to one's mind.

"People may hear your words, but they feel your attitude."

John C. Maxwell

Week Three

Negotiation

"Relationships are a constant negotiation and balance."

Claire Danes

Negotiation may involve some discussion aimed at reaching an agreement between two or more people. It may take some to-and-froing before all parties are happy with the result. Negotiation is a useful skill to have in life as it can help us to resolve conflicts or solve problems. Teenagers who have good negotiation skills may also become more independent, needing less help from an adult when faced with conflict. Good negotiators often need to listen to others and be flexible. Indian philosopher Maharishi Mahesh Yogi has an interesting opinion of negotiation, saying, "To resolve problems through negotiation is a very childish approach."

On my first trip around Southeast Asia, I would love bartering with the street vendors or business owners. I was told that this negotiation was part of their culture, and they respected the travellers who did bargain. Sometimes, after much haggling, when we had agreed on a price, I would leave them with some extra money. On a trip to Vietnam with Daisy a few years ago, I bargained for a puffer vest. When we got home, I found out that it had no down filling in it at all as had been promised. The vest was full of synthetic material that hardly kept me warm.

With your teen, discuss which activity you would like to do from the following list then negotiate until you agree on which one to do.

- ★ Have your parent ask you to do something. You need to reply with, "I will do what you have asked once you have …" Fill the gap. Discuss what you discovered.

- ★ Eat something healthy. Then ask if you can eat something not so healthy, like this: "I've just eaten an apple and a pear. Could I please have a biscuit now?"

- ★ Do something kind for someone. Then ask if they will do something kind for you in return.

- ★ When you are asked to do a job around the house, see if you can negotiate to complete it at a different time. You may like to see if you can adjust or change the task instead.

- ★ During dinner, see if you can trade some food with someone else at the table.

- ★ Play Monopoly together. Are there any other games you can play that involve negotiation?

- ★ Find a book that you have read before and see if you can trade it with a friend for a book that they have read.

- ★ Your parent must offer to do something kind for you. You cannot say yes immediately, no matter how good the offer may seem. The challenge is for you to negotiate for more.

- ★ Go to the op shop or a garage sale and find something you like. Ask how much the item is then offer them a little less. See what happens.

- ★ Ask your parent to do something. They need to negotiate and adjust your request. How successful were they?

Sim

When I was riding home, I noticed a dog following me. I wondered why but kept on riding. It wasn't until I got home that I realised that it was hungry, and it could smell the pies I had bought for lunch that were on my bike rack. The dog was massive. It was a German Shepherd – Great Dane cross. I waited for a while thinking he'd leave but he didn't so in the end I gave some of my pie that I'd saved. Immediately we formed a bond, and I knew that I wanted to keep him. But I also knew my parents. We lived in a quiet suburb and had no front fence. We never closed the back gate until he came. My parents were not dog people. I knew that they would worry about the dog barking at night and annoying the neighbours. Somehow, I managed to convince my parents to keep the dog and I named him James. That beautiful free spirit who took my thoughts away. I promised to take care of James and do whatever it took to ensure that he stayed with us. We bought a side gate, but James would often escape and turn up at the local school or the dog catcher would return him with a fine that my parents would pay. Then his barking was beginning to annoy the neighbours, and I thought that he would be taken away. But I wanted to keep my dog so much that my parents eventually decided that if he was to stay, they would have his voice box removed. This ensured that he stayed with me for a while longer, but he was this huge dog that was nearly as tall as me that barked like a chihuahua. No fence or person ever stole his free spirit. James helped me to learn about freedom and boundaries.

"There's no road map on how to raise a family: it's always an enormous negotiation."

Meryl Streep

Week Four
Sense of Humour

*"Humour is by far the most significant
activity of the human brain."*

Edward de Bono

This is a very important and serious life skill. And I mean really serious. What would life be like if we couldn't have a laugh? A little giggle or one of those laughs we have with a friend when you can't stop laughing with each other and your stomach hurts. "Please stop. No more." But the laughing continues. People who have a great sense of humour may often be surrounded by others. They can appear to be magnetic. There have been loads of studies into the benefits of laughter and how it does great stuff to your brain. But who needs studies? We all know what it's like to laugh and have fun. Laughing can be a great way for us to cope with stress and from which we can also gain many health benefits. Apparently, some scientists believe that it can lower blood pressure and aid muscle relaxation. Mahatma Ghandi was quoted as saying 'If I had no sense of humour, I would long ago have committed suicide.' But all this sense of humour business sounds way to serious to me!

I met Zdrav when the family moved, and I started at a new school. He came up, introduced himself, and we instantly hit it off. Zdrav is one of the funniest people I know. His humour is very immature, but I cannot help laughing when I'm in his company or talking on the phone. When he calls, my family all know who I'm talking to within a few moments, as I don't behave in that way with anyone else. Zdrav always makes me laugh and I always feel better after talking and laughing with him.

Have a look at the following list of things to do to help boost your family's sense of humour at home. Choose your favourite one or two and have a good laugh along the way.

- ★ Think about something funny that happened to you when you were younger. Tell your family about it and why it still makes you laugh.
- ★ Go to the library and get some joke books and tell jokes to each other. You could look for jokes on Google or YouTube instead.
- ★ Have a staring competition – the person who keeps a straight face the longest wins.
- ★ Watch a comedy movie or television series together with the family.
- ★ Talk about funny people you know. What makes them funny? Why do you laugh at them? Talk about things that they do to make you laugh.
- ★ Look through a family photo album and find photos that make you laugh. What is it about those photos? Is the photo funny or does it bring back a funny memory?
- ★ Make up some really bad 'Dad Jokes'. Any joke that gets a laugh gets one point.
- ★ Get a newspaper and draw on the pictures to make them look funny. Can you get others to laugh?
- ★ Put on some music and do some silly dancing together.
- ★ Go to a local comedy club and watch some live stand-up comedy. You may like to watch some stand-up comedy together on catch up TV or YouTube.

Hugh

At high school, I was often in trouble because I was always trying to get a laugh from others. Some teachers understood me, and others didn't. I remember getting good marks or grades from the teachers who I had good relationships with. But my report card was bad with the teachers who I didn't get along with. When I was younger, I remember Mum chasing me around the house, eventually catching me then hitting me on the bum which broke the wooden spoon! So, in a woodwork lesson, I made a wooden spoon and gave it to my Mum.

"The problem with having a sense of humour is often that people you use it on aren't in a very good mood."

Lou Holtz

December: Self-Management

Week One

Patience

"Nature does not hurry, yet everything is accomplished."

Lao Tsu

Patience may be defined as the ability to accept delays while remaining calm and without becoming annoyed. It may help us to persevere with something when we experience difficulties, to continue without complaining. I have noticed that patient people tend to be calmer and more relaxed. They may arrive somewhere a few minutes later than someone who raced to be on time, however they tend to arrive in a more peaceful state of mind. Perhaps these people may be present more quickly once they do arrive, whereas the person who arrived on time after rushing might take a while to calm down? When we are patient, we tend to be able to problem solve in a more relaxed and methodical manner. We may take our time to think of different solutions to problems or challenges we face. As they say, 'patience is a virtue'.

As a kid, I used to work many jobs and I'd save my money. I decided to buy a new television and VCR for my bedroom. I didn't ask my mum, as I thought she'd say no. Because I couldn't wait for the weekend, I told Mum that I was sick, and didn't go to school. Instead, I took the tram to the shops, and spent my money on the two new items. I carried them back home on another tram, set them up and watched TV for the afternoon. When Mum came home, I was so excited that I showed her. I was rather surprised when she became angry with me for lying to her and taking the day off school. What was I thinking?

Some of the following ideas might help improve the skill of patience. Carefully choose one to try together this week.

- ★ After dinner, see how long you can sit still in silence without communicating with anyone. The person who lasts the longest is the winner, and the person who communicates first gets to clean the kitchen.
- ★ Have a discussion with the family in silence by writing down what you want to say. You can only use one piece of paper and one pencil. Consider using your non-preferred writing hand.
- ★ Play a board or card game together. Take your time and think carefully when it is your turn.
- ★ Everyone draws a crazy scribble on a blank piece of paper. Pass it to someone else and have them carefully colour in each part of the scribble.
- ★ Get an egg and see how long it takes you to balance it on the table standing on its end.
- ★ Sit in the lounge and read together. Someone might like to read to everyone else.
- ★ Build a house of cards. How high can you build it?
- ★ Sit around together and quietly start to breathe deeply together. Close your eyes and notice your breathing. As you begin to relax, see if you can breathe more deeply. See how long you can continue to breathe deeply with your eyes closed. What did you notice?
- ★ Stack some coins on top of each other, end to end. How many coins high can you stack? Try the same with some other objects.

★ Talk about all the things where patience is an absolute must. Are there any situations where you find yourself becoming impatient?

Ronan

I'd been dreaming of doing a trip around Australia since I started high school. At different points in time, my dad would tell me stories of his trip around Australia when he was younger such as when his Kombi van caught on fire or when he backpacked around the centre and up north. After finishing school, my mate and I got a van and spent a couple of months working and kitting it out. We caught the ferry to the mainland and started our adventure. After a few months, we were staying on remote cliff campsite right up north. We hadn't passed a shop in a while so our supplies were starting to run low. We decided to try to catch our dinner as we'd heard that there were mackerel in the reefs off the cliffs. It was getting later in the afternoon, and we'd spent quite a few hours fishing without any luck. Thankfully, we had a trevally in our fridge that we caught a couple of days earlier, so we gave up fishing for the day and pan fried it with some butter. We spent the whole next day trying to catch anything. We could see some queenfish taunting us in the reef, and we had lost all our lures to catch them. Once again, we caught nothing. We had to cook the last of the trevally for dinner, but we were starting to get desperate. We awoke on the third day and decided to give it one last shot, but we had to do something different. We netted some live bait and used that with no success. As I was fishing on the rocks, I noticed a lure that someone had probably lost, sitting on the edge of the water as the tide had gone out. I gave it to my friend as I was still using the live bait. The live bait was attracting the fish, but they still weren't biting. My mate cast the lure into where the school of fish were swimming around the live bait, and I heard him yelling out for help. It was challenging to get the queenfish out of the water as the rocks were slippery to stand on and he couldn't get down to the edge of the water. That night, dinner tasted so good.

"The two most powerful warriors are patience and time."

Leo Tolstoy

Week Two

Staying Calm

"Mistakes and pressure are inevitable; the secret
to getting past them is to stay calm."

Travis Bradberry

Remaining calm when things start to get busy or stressful is a wonderful skill to have. It may mean we appear not to be nervous, angry or to show any other strong emotions. Staying calm might be when we are able to take a breath, step back and evaluate the situation. By remaining calm and considering all the options when faced with challenges, we can save time and be more efficient. It may even help us to solve problems that others find difficult when they become flustered or confused. Some might say that this is the ability to think clearly when placed under pressure.

I am usually a fairly calm person, but when I go to the footy, or watch it on TV, I let loose. I love watching the AFL, particularly when my team are playing. I yell out, whether I'm at the match or sitting in the lounge watching. I get so emotionally involved, that it takes me a while to calm down when the game is finished. When the new season is approaching, I will usually get excited, hoping for a positive start, but for a long time, my team has underperformed. Maybe things will be different this year.

Choose something from this list to do with your teen so they may learn to remain calm when placed in tricky situations.

- ★ When you are feeling angry, how do you cool down and not blow your top? Share some strategies you use that help you calm down when you are starting to feel this way.

- ★ Share what makes you mad, then act it out just like when it actually does happen. What did you notice? What did others notice? How did your body feel?

- ★ Take very deep and long breaths. What do you notice about your body? What about your mood?

- ★ Listen to some different music together. What type of music helps you to relax and calm down. Are there some genres of music that do the opposite?

- ★ Play a board game or card game together. Notice your body and how it changes throughout the game. Talk about your body sensations when you have finished. Now try a different game and see if there are any different sensations that you experience.

- ★ Ask some of your friends or extended family how they remain calm when things get busy, or they become stressed. Make a list of any ideas that you think you could use if you started to become stressed.

- ★ During the day, go outside and lie on the ground and look up at the clouds. What do you notice about your body? Listen to the sounds around you. Do any sounds make your body relax? What other sounds do you hear and what other sensations do you notice in your body?

★ Some people say that when they feel angry, they 'see red'. What colours describe other emotions? Which emotions would you prefer to feel when you are getting angry and what colour could they be? If you think you are starting to feel angry, what might happen if you think of a different colour? Try it out and talk about what happened.

★ Go for a walk together and notice how you feel? What happens if you walk at a brisk pace? What about a slow pace? Could a walk help you if you were starting to feel upset? What other types of exercise might help you calm down? Discuss.

★ If you start to feel annoyed, what would happen if you made a fart noise? Are there any other noises you could create that would shift you from being annoyed to another emotion? Try making some different noises to each other and see what happens. What happens if you pull funny faces?

Rick

Early 1998. 18 years old. School is over. I feel a little anxious. My world is changing.

I split up with my girlfriend. She makes the call. We had been dating since late 1996. I am confused and don't yet quite understand why. I visit her at home to try and talk about things. She is different, aloof, dismissive. Words I would not have used to comprehend it back then, but age and experience assist me to understand it now. I make the decision to leave and walk home alone in the early evening – from Highton to Grovedale. A rather lengthy sojourn. But I recall thinking that it was required to help me survive. Halfway home, a large car pulls up alongside me. Three boys inside the car. All boys from my high school class. At least two of them, friends since primary school. One of them had been rumoured to be seeing my girlfriend in the later stages of our time together but I had left it alone and not believed it. This boy instantly became verbally violent towards me and knew where I had been that day. He ranted, yelled, and threatened me with physical violence. I stood alone on the footpath without an ounce of support. I recall quietly denying accusations that were outrageous and totally untrue. Meanwhile, the two other guys in the car simply sat and watched it unfold. I was so frightened and yet felt a sense of shame. I ran part of the way home. That night, I didn't know where to put my rage and despair, so I punched a hole in my bedroom wall – put a calendar over the hole and left it. I can't recall who I confided in, but I did tell my parents at some point. Looking back, I am proud of my young self for not responding with anger or threats of violence. Yet the experience was visceral and still haunts me to a degree even today. If I see any of the people involved (and I have done over the years) I get a physical sensation of dread, anger, and fright among others. It devastated me.

> "One important reason to stay calm is that calm parents hear more. Low-key, accepting parents are the ones whose children keep talking."
>
> Mary Pipher

Week Three

Stress Management

"You need to be able to manage stress because hard times will come, and a positive outlook is what gets you through."

Marie Osmond

Stress could be defined as something that causes the body to become tense in some way. Being able to manage stress or situations that may cause us to become stressed is a positive attribute. Many scientists believe that reducing stress can help to improve both physical and mental health. They also suggest that it can help to prolong life. Stress has been linked to anxiety and depression. It has also been said that stress can even contribute to making you cranky! Who would have thought? Managing our stress levels may help us to create a calm environment around us; a place where others may like to be with us. Managing stress may also help us get more done by keeping a clear and focused direction. We may find that not only do we get more done, but we are able to create more time to do other things that we may really enjoy.

I still have nightmares at night of the times that I was working in hospitality. The food won't come out of the kitchen quickly enough. I can't get to all the tables to get everyone's order. Customers keep coming in and I keep falling behind. When I eventually wake up, usually in a sweat, at that moment in the middle of the night, I do not want to go back into hospitality.

Calmly choose your favourite from the following list to try together at home to help learn to manage your stress levels.

- ★ Make a list of some things you need to do. Next, put them in order from most to least important. Now, just do the first thing on the top of your list, but nothing else. How did you feel when you completed just one thing?

- ★ Try some simple meditation together. You may wish to search YouTube or Google.

- ★ Find a good place to sit away from any distractions and close your eyes. Listen to the sounds around you. Focus on your feet and how they feel. Slowly, work your way up your body, noticing how each part of your body is feeling. When you get to the top of your body, think about the smells that you notice?

- ★ Tell each other jokes that you know or borrow a joke book from the library. Were any of the jokes funny? What did you notice if you heard a funny joke?

- ★ Have someone in your family give you a back or foot tickle, or a gentle shoulder massage. How did it make you feel?

- ★ Go for a slow family walk together around the neighbourhood or to the local park. Consider watching the sunset together.

- ★ Do some yoga together as a family. Try searching on YouTube for some basic yoga sessions.

- ★ Play a board game or card game together and try not to win.

- ★ Download a free meditation app, such as 'Smiling Mind', and see what you discover.

- ★ Go to the local pool, river or beach and have a paddle and play in the water.

Tim

When I was about sixteen, I decided to play cricket for the local club because I thought it might be a fun thing to do. I had never played cricket before apart from hitting the ball in the street with my brothers. I started training with the club and they said they needed players, so I signed up. I bought all the gear and was a little nervous to begin with. I was selected for third grade, which was the lowest grade for our club. The captain placed me at 11th position in the batting order, so it was easy to say that I was the worst batsman in the club. I think

I was just there to make up the numbers. For the first four weeks or so, I made a total of no more than four runs, which is about what I expected. I was nervous and scared and I had no idea of what I was doing. Four runs in four games are almost not worth mentioning. On the fifth game when I went into bat, the whole team was out except for myself and my partner. I'm sure everyone was thinking that the game would be over in a matter of minutes. I hit a few good shots and my confidence started to grow. The fast bowlers didn't seem to scare me anymore. I then hit a couple of fours before hitting one in the air which the fielder dropped. My partner and I just kept on batting and he made a century. We felt invincible and a win was now a possibility. I hit a ball into the air and unfortunately this time I was caught after making a massive 40 runs, so we were out. Once we made it back to the club rooms, we found out that we had set a record eleventh wicket partnership for the club.

"Being in control of your life and having realistic expectations about your day-to-day challenges are the keys to stress management, which is perhaps the most important ingredient to living a happy, healthy and rewarding life."

Marilu Henner

Week Four
Compassion and Kindness

"If you want others to be happy, practice compassion.
If you want to be happy, practice compassion."

Dalai Lama

Compassionate people may see the suffering of others and want to help them in some way. The word comes from the Latin 'compassio', which means to suffer together. The Dalai Lama suggests that compassion is the key to happiness. Other benefits may include a boost to our health and longevity as well as uplifting others around us. Some believe being compassionate can even make us more attractive!

When dealing with friendship issues children have in the yard, all I ask is that they are kind to each other. It doesn't really matter if they are friends or that they play together, as long as they are kind to each other. Often children forget to be kind and they make mistakes. I'll ask them to be kind by apologising, then ask them to remember to be kind to each other in future. Kindness helps to teach compassion.

Here are a few fun ideas to try together to help foster compassion and kindness. Choose one from the list to do this week with your teenager.

★ Phone a relative or friend that you haven't talked to in a while.

- ★ One person acts out a mood that they may not normally like such as sadness, being tired, upset or lonely. Someone else notices their mood and helps them to feel better.
- ★ Find some clothes that you don't want anymore and donate them to a charity or give them to an op shop.
- ★ Think about someone you have noticed who hasn't been as happy as they usually are. Do something kind for them to cheer them up.
- ★ Pick some flowers from your garden and give them to a stranger.
- ★ Consider sponsoring a child from an underprivileged country.
- ★ Think about someone that lives near you, who might need some help. Cook them a meal or help them in the garden for an hour or so.
- ★ Role play some of the following situations: a friend looks lonely, one of the family feels unwell, someone is tired at the end of the day, you notice a stranger fall over and hurt themselves. How do you show kindness in these situations?
- ★ Next time you are at work or school, talk to someone you normally don't talk to.
- ★ Cook a meal or a sweet treat and give it to someone else.

Sue

During secondary school, I had a really close friend who I'd spend a lot of time with. We'd always sit together, catch the train to and from school together and would always walk from the train station to the park on the way back from school, and then phone each other as soon as we were home as we had a lot of private in-jokes between us. There was a girl at school who was a little older than us and she looked a tiny bit different. We laughed about her behind her back, and we made up an unkind name for her. We even invented a special noise that we'd make each time we saw her at school. We thought it was so funny. My friend and I never talked to her, and we didn't even know her name. We were really careless and lacked any thought about her. I reckon we knew it was mean but that didn't stop us. We kept doing it because it amused us. The crazy thing was that I was not brought up to behave like this. As an adult, I feel embarrassed about my behaviour and I can't even fathom how we could have made fun about the way somebody looked.

"Love and compassion are necessities, not luxuries. Without them humanity cannot survive."

Dalai Lama

Acknowledgements

This book was written as a gesture of my love for my wife Sandi, and our children Daisy, Finn, and Monty. I am truly grateful to have them in my life. I would also like to thank my extended family, friends, and colleagues for their support with everything I do. A special shout out to Mum and Dad.

There are many people who have helped put this book together and in countless ways. Firstly, thanks to those who shared their stories. It was a pleasure spending time with you, and I have learnt so much from you. Your stories have inspired me, and I am sure they will inspire others. Thanks for being who you are. Thanks to Sandi, Sally, and Jak for your editing and feedback. I am grateful to Sylvie for helping me to get started with my first book. Linda, Julie, Fran, Tracey, and Sue, I thank you for your support with the workshops, webinars, and conferences. I would also like to thank Ted for your passion with inclusion. Alicia, I feel extremely grateful for your support and your belief in me. It has been a pleasure working with you and you have made everything so easy. Thanks also to Tess for the cover design and for the bees. Cheers to Nick for your amazing photos – working with you is always such a pleasure. Thanks also to Sarah for the extremely thorough final edit.

All of you have helped with this book and helped me to be the person I am today – thankyou.

Andy McNeilly

Acknowledgements

This book was written as a gesture of my love for my wife Sandi, and our children Daisy, Finn, and Monty. I am truly grateful to have them in my life. I would also like to thank my extended family, friends, and colleagues for their support with everything I do. A special shout out to Mum and Dad.

There are many people who have helped put this book together and in countless ways. Firstly, thanks to those who shared their stories. It was a pleasure spending time with you, and I have learnt so much from you. Your stories have inspired me, and I am sure they will inspire others. Thanks for being who you are. Thanks to Sandi, Sally, and Jak for your editing and feedback. I am grateful to Sylvie for helping me to get started with my first book. Linda, Julie, Fran, Tracey, and Sue, I thank you for your support with the workshops, webinars, and conferences. I would also like to thank Ted for your passion with inclusion. Alicia, I feel extremely grateful for your support and your belief in me. It has been a pleasure working with you and you have made everything so easy. Thanks also to Tess for the cover design and for the bees. Cheers to Nick for your amazing photos – working with you is always such a pleasure. Thanks also to Sarah for the extremely thorough final edit.

All of you have helped with this book and helped me to be the person I am today – thankyou.

Andy McNeilly

About the Author

Andy McNeilly is an educator, speaker, coach, author and most importantly a husband and father. He has worked in education for nearly twenty years, including primary school children and adult education. Andy has extensive experience in wellbeing as well as social and emotional learning for children and adults.

Connecting with Your Teens is Andy's second book. Andy's first book, *Connecting with Your Kids* offers practical advice and fun opportunities for families to build skills and connect, leading to a fuller life for everyone.

Andy and his wife Sandi are the parents of three amazing kids: Daisy, Finn, and Monty. It is here in his family where Andy has learnt the importance of having strong, connected, and nurturing relationships. Andy intends to continue writing books for educators and organisations about building connected relationships.

www.ingramcontent.com/pod-product-compliance
Lightning Source LLC
Chambersburg PA
CBHW081617100526
44590CB00021B/3486

www.ingramcontent.com/pod-product-compliance
Lightning Source LLC
Chambersburg PA
CBHW081617100526
44590CB00021B/3486